DEDICATION

To my partner: the great listener.

Shakespeare Short Guides

Othello

analysis, notes and exemplar essays

E.N Cartwright

CONTENTS

ACKNOWLEDGMENTS

All my students, who have taught me as much for this as I have taught them.

Introduction

What's expected of me in this exam?

Well, hello, exam candidate.

I'm sure you've bought this purely to help you understand Shakespeare just a little better and not, of course, to cram an exemplar essay into your head a few days before the exam. Eek!

Now, the first thing to remember is that your teacher has given you specific advice for your exam, and she/he knows you much better than this book. So: FOLLOW THEIR ADVICE FIRST!

Do what they want you to do, take good notes, and listen to their feedback to improve. You have most likely had lots of attempts and feedback on your essay writing skills. Follow what your teacher wants you to do and use this guide to add to that.

Now, I have taught many kinds of exams to many pupils across many countries. Here is some general advice that I would bet applies to any exam:

- There is a time limit. It may be the essay is the only thing you need to do or part of a bigger paper, but you need to learn how to manage your time.

- You must write a complete essay – something half-finished scores less than a short but finished essay.

- You must show knowledge of the whole text (beginning, middle and end) to score top marks. A

3

marker wants to see that you understand it all.

- You must give **references** and **quotations**. These are the basis for any response.

- You should name **techniques** of English Lit (metaphor, simile, word choice, etc). This is usually in a mark scheme, looked for by markers.

- An introduction and a conclusion are rarely in a mark scheme but are expected in a longer piece of critical writing. If your exam doesn't call for a formal 'essay' then these may not to be needed but be guided by your teacher.

- The exam will usually provide a question/**task**. Sometimes tasks are genre specific and, so, you must choose 'Drama' since you are covering *Othello* which is a play. Oh, and put the number of the question – this helps your marker.

- Don't write everything you know – choose what answers the task. Be selective, and don't just write a plot summary. That's not what a critical response is. Yes, show knowledge of what happens but a critical essay is something much more.

- The quickest way to do the above is to **repeat the key words** from the task itself. If it asks about a "character you feel sympathy for" then say the word "sympathy" at least twice a paragraph.

- There is no set 'way' to do an essay. You may have been taught TARTS, BAPs, PEAs, PEARs, PCQEs, and on and on, but it's rare for an exam board to have a preference.

  All these acronyms are just a teacher's way of trying to get you to do the following: show you know the play; show you know some quotations; show you know some analysis: and link all that information to the task give in the exam.

Othello

Context

Who was Shakespeare and why did he write this rollercoaster play?

A writer whom English teachers love. He died a long time ago.

There's actually very little else you need to know about Shakespeare's actual life other than that. English Literature exams aren't testing you on your historical knowledge and English Literature mark scheme rarely reward this.

But sometimes **social and historical context** is in the mark scheme. This isn't the same as facts about Shakespeare. This is information about the setting, writer or political/social climate at the time of the production of the drama which helps us understand it better or in a different way. This information is especially useful if you are looking for that A or top band mark.

So ...

The first thing we need to make sure is that we have some understanding of the racial terms of the play. Othello is described as a 'Moor', a Jacobean term (i.e. used at the time of King James 1st) for darker than European white. But some writers at the time of Shakespeare describe the "white Moors" of Northern Africa on the Mediterranean coasts or areas such as Turkey. Yes, Shakespeare overtly refers to Othello's blackness several times in the play, but the actual racial differences between Othello and the other characters may be less pronounced than a modern audience has come to expect.

Shakespeare also stole much of the play's plot and narrative. It was actually a common device of Shakespeare to read something that inspired his imagination and for him to then reimagine events. In this case, an Italian story written in 1565 by Cinthio. This original tale had the basic elements of Shakespeare's (such as a Moorish general tricked by his second in command into believing his wife has been unfaithful) but Shakespeare has added characters to create a stronger drama. His writing also elevates the character of Iago into a world-renowned arch-villain. Shakespeare has taken this kind of 'inspiration' from fellow writers in a number of other plays, but the mark of his genius isn't in his creation, but what he does with these characters once he is writing them. Shakespeare's intellect and power as a writer creates something wonderful and still being performed almost five hundred years later!

The play itself isn't actually 'set at the time of Shakespeare' but the narrative setting is slightly early: just after the Battle of Lepanto. This was a battle between the Christian Venetians (whom Othello fought for) and the Muslim Ottomans (and Othello used to be a Muslim). This backdrop creates a sense of danger and violence to the play but is also reflective of the racial and social tensions of the play. The struggle between Christianity and Islam, between white Venetians and the Moorish Turks, is represented in the battle between Iago and Othello and the internal battle with Othello about finding his rightful place and claiming his heritage.

Now this **social and historical knowledge** isn't all that you need to know to understand the play – and, in fact, you could probably understand it quite well without knowing it – but it does add dimension and flavour to any critical response should you choose to include it. The use of this kind of information tends to be the marker of a higher end candidate as it shows a deepness of thought about *Othello* that many other candidates lack, especially if you can weave it into your answer without it taking away from your actual knowledge of the play itself.

And that's the key: it's always extra!

The Text Itself

Remember it's a play!

Before we go much further you just need to remember one clear and distinct thing – this is a play/drama.

Why is that important?

Well, markers rarely see essays on Shakespeare that remember it is designed to be watched and not to be read. You get a few extra marks for understanding that idea. For example, acknowledging that there are actors, sets, special effects, stage directions, etc. These all show that you understand the **genre** of the thing that you have studied. This is rarely done and can make your essay stand out from the crowd.

These things also affect our understanding of the play. For example, almost all presentations of Othello as a character have him played him black actors to foreground the race of the character as important. But directors can also make unusual choices to affect the play. One example of this is a version of *Othello* that was staged with an all-black cast apart from the character of Othello who was played by a white actor. This kept the racial tension within the script but changed the dynamics.

Plays can change from how they are written basically!

Common mistakes because it's a drama:

- The person who wrote it is Shakespeare, the writer or the dramatist.

  It's **not** the poet or the maker, for example.

- The text is called the text, the play, or the drama.

  It is **not** the book or the film. You may have used a book or film to help you study the play, but you are writing an essay on the play.

- The audience or the viewer reacts.

  It is **not** the reader. You may have read sections of the play, but essays discuss influence on audience.

- You need to know the difference between **dialogue** and **stage directions**.

  - ✓ Dialogue: these are the words written on the page by Shakespeare and designed to be learned and said out-loud by the actors.

  - ✓ Stage directions: these are the instructions written by Shakespeare about sets, movement of actors, special effects. These are not meant to be reader to the audience, although you can analyse them in your essay.

    Shakespeare (because he directed his own plays) doesn't use many stage directions. He didn't need to write instructions down – he would just say them to the actors himself. They are usually printed on the page in *italics.*

9

The Plot and Characters

Eh, what happens?

Now, this is a very complicated play. A lot happens but, to cheer you up a bit, you don't need to know every line and every 'why' and every action. No exam board can expect you (only a student!) to have knowledge that many English Literature graduates do not have – especially as this is written in some of the most complicated language in history.

What they do expect is for you to have an overview understanding. They might not expect you to know what happens in Act 1 Scene 5 line 5, but they do expect you to know that Iago manipulates Othello into certain actions at certain points. So, here's a basic overview ....

'Back of the book' summary

After a decisive victory in battle, Iago is a Venetian soldier who is passed over for promotion by Othello, a Moorish general who has reached the pinnacle of his career. Othello is beloved by the people of Venice for this victory and this also eats at Iago who wants revenge. Therefore, Iago convinces Othello that his wife, Desdemona, is being unfaithful. This results in Othello killing Desdemona, Iago killing his own wife, Iago being arrested, and Othello killing himself.

The Main Cast

Othello, a Moorish general in the Venetian military

Desdemona, Othello's wife; daughter of Brabantio, although Brabantio does not know Othello and Desdemona are married at the start of the play

Iago, Othello's trusted, but jealous and traitorous ensign

Cassio, Othello's loyal and most beloved captain

Bianca, Cassio's lover

Emilia, Iago's wife and Desdemona's maidservant

Brabantio, Venetian senator and Desdemona's father

Roderigo, a Venetian in love with Desdemona

Act 1

Iago confesses to hating Othello to Roderigo primarily because Othello promoted Cassio over Iago, yet there are also racist overtones to this hatred. He also knows that Desdemona and Othello have married without telling her father, Brabantio, so go to his window to tell him what has happened. Iago is aware this will anger Brabantio, a powerful Venetian man, and Iago makes it worse by using very sexual language to Brabantio.

Iago then goes to Othello to tell him that Brabantio knows about his marriage, but Othello seems unconcerned. The Duke of Venice summons Othello due to an expected attack by the Turkish Ottoman empire while Brabantio arrives to arrest Othello for using witchcraft to steal his daughter.

In front of the Duke, Othello describes telling Desdemona stories of his life to make her love him and Desdemona is called, confirming that she loves Othello truly. Brabantio has no choice but to accept the marriage, but he seems unhappy.

Iago uses a **soliloquy** to further detail his mischief.

Act 2

Various ships arrive at Cyprus, the site of the expected attack. They find a storm has destroyed the Turkish fleet. When Desdemona's ship arrives, Cassio praises her highly – which Iago uses to convince Roderigo, who loves Desdemona, that she is already cheating on Othello with Cassio. He tries to encourage Roderigo to challenge Cassio to a duel. Yet, the audience see Desdemona and Othello arrive on separate ships and are joyous to see each other again – highlighting their true love.

Othello and his men decide to hold a party to celebrate this victory over the Turks (and Othello and Desdemona's marriage). At the party, Iago encourages Cassio to drink, even though the younger man makes it clear that he gets easily drunk. Iago also provokes Roderigo to attempt to fight Cassio. Montano, a governor in Cyprus, attempts to stop the fight but drunken Cassio ends up injuring Montano instead.

When Othello comes back, he is enraged at the scenes he sees and he trusts Iago, expecting the man to tell him the truth. Iago claims that he does not wish to speak badly of Cassio but tells Othello of what has happened. Cassio loses his rank when Othello demotes him, and Cassio's drunken state means that he remembers very little of what happened. He is also really concerned about losing the good reputation he has built up and Othello's good opinion of him.

Iago is not done though and convinces Cassio to attempt to get Desdemona to intercede on his behalf with Othello, while Iago tells the audience that he will also speak to Othello to provoke jealousy. Iago is setting up Desdemona to look like she is protecting Cassio because she is having an affair. This also allows Iago to get further revenge on Cassio, someone that he does not like because he feels betrayed by him.

Roderigo eventually returns and seems annoyed about the plan and its collapse – remember he wanted to fight Cassio – but Iago assures him that it is working. Iago doesn't seem to have a specific goal other than just upsetting those around him.

Act 3

Cassio seeks Emilia's (Iago's wife and Desdemona's maidservant) advice and intercession in getting Desdemona's help – which Desdemona readily provides, assuring Cassio that she will try to get Othello and Cassio back on friendly terms. The audience see that this is motivated by Desdemona's love for Othello and her desire to make him happy. Her goodness only highlights the wrongs done to her.

Iago begins to manipulate the situation (with information from his wife) so that Othello catches the end of Cassio and Desdemona's conversation – and Iago makes Othello think that there was something illicit in the conversation. They catch the very end and Cassio walking away, with Iago making Othello think that Cassio was hiding from them as if he and Desdemona were doing something wrong.

Iago then builds up his language in this act, starting off creating Othello's suspicion slowly but more and more building it up as the idea takes hold of Othello's mind. There is a sense in which Iago is both creating the suspicion – but also revealing a dark side that was already inside of Othello. Othello seems trapped in a web – and he also trusts his 'friend' Iago – and so his suspicions build and begin to take over his thinking.

This actually has a physical effect on Othello, who begins to complain about a headache and being unable to think straight. At one-point Desdemona rubs Othello's head to soothe him with a special handkerchief which was a gift from him to her. But, on leaving the stage, she drops it. Emilia picks it up to give to Iago, who has been trying to get Emilia to steal it for a long time.

The scene ends with Othello coming back on stage, demanding proof from Iago. Iago claims to have heard Cassio talking in his sleep about the affair and that Cassio has been bragging about the affair to the soldiers – including using Othello's love-token of a handkerchief given to Desdemona.

Othello says he will kill Desdemona and demands that Iago kill Cassio.

Act 4

Iago goads and controls Othello, this time claiming that he knows Cassio and Desdemona have had sex. This causes Othello to have an epileptic fit, and Iago then makes fun of him. Cassio briefly comes on stage to see this, and Iago claims this is common for Othello and they have to let the fit run its course.

Once Othello comes round, Iago makes him hide while Iago speaks to Cassio about his relationship to Bianca. Othello is unable to clearly make out the conversation – and Iago carefully controls the content – so thinks that Cassio is discussing an afraid with Desdemona instead. Othello decides to kill Desdemona that evening.

Just then Desdemona enters with a Venetian nobleman who gives them instructions to come home. Desdemona tries to discuss Cassio and repair the relationship with Othello, but this angers Othello so much that he strikes Desdemona. The nobleman is shocked at this behaviour, and Iago hints that Othello is going mad and is out of control.

Othello then confronts both Emilia and Desdemona, but his ranting and raving does not mention Cassio specifically, instead it is non-specifically calling Desdemona a "whore". She strongly denies it, as does Emilia. Iago gets Othello to leave the room and promises the women he will fix the situation.

Roderigo shouts at Iago as he paid Iago in jewels to help him win Desdemona, but this has not happened. Iago manages to convince Roderigo to kill Cassio to prevent Desdemona from leaving for Venice with Othello.

As Desdemona gets ready for bed, she discusses her confusion with Emilia. She describes having a song stuck in her head that her mother used to sing about a woman who loved a man who went mad. This foreshadows and ironically parallels the events of the play. Emilia assures Desdemona that she believes her and that it is the fault of men/husbands for not understanding wives better.

Act 5

Phew – nearly there! But this is a long one ...

Iago's two plots are now woven together. The first part takes place when Roderigo attacks Cassio, who is a better fighter and manages to wound Roderigo. During the fight, Iago creeps out and stabs Cassio in the leg. Cassio cries out, which acts as a sign to Othello that Iago has done his part in the plan in killing Cassio for him and is signal for him to kill Desdemona. Iago then secretly returns and kills Roderigo, who is a witness to Iago's own crimes in the situation.

Othello arrives in Desdemona's chamber and she is asleep. He gives her kiss, showing some semblance of the love that he had for her. He initially refuses to spill her blood (i.e. stab her) but is determined that she must die. She wakes up and he demands she tell him the truth about Cassio, and, in her honesty, she refuses – so he suffocates her.

Emilia hears the commotion and runs into the room, seeing her mistress dead on the bed. Othello immediately confesses to his crime but says it is because she was false and had cheated on him. He also implicates Iago, telling Emilia that it was her husband who had told him everything. Emilia is horrified to hear of Iago's involvement, and she is beginning to realise the part that she has played in everything. Others come into the room, including Iago. He tries to make his wife be quiet, but she refuses, revealing that she stole the handkerchief. Iago is revealed as behind it all – and he stabs his wife, is stabbed by Othello (not fatally), and runs.

Iago is soon brought back, captured, and arrested by Cassio and others. When asked why he had undertaken this, Iago refuses to explain his motives and, in fact, says that he will never speak again. Othello is also arrested for the murder of his wife, but Othello stabs himself asking to not be remembered too harshly for the events.

He kisses Desdemona and dies.

Main Themes

Yeah, but what is it all about?

A theme is an idea or message crafted by the writer (or rising out of the text) that engages the audience to think. It is an idea or message not just about the events or characters, but something wider – it is a philosophical, social or moral point about the whole world or society.

It is often linked to the 'message' of the play or what the audience is supposed to 'learn from' the play. These aren't exactly what a theme are, but they are a good starting point to begin to wrap your head around what it is.

Ultimately, it is the 'point' of the play; the thing we, the viewer, are supposed to 'take' away from having watched it.

Themes are important parts of texts – but are difficult!

Understanding of theme is important if you are looking to enter those top bands and get those top grades. Thematic understanding – and theme-based essays – allow you to discuss the 'big ideas' of the text and, therefore, allow you to show how smart you are.

It is also usually in the mark scheme. What you have learned/taken away from the text (what has stuck with you) is usually part of the mark scheme. We can acknowledge this in the conclusion, sometimes as simple as "This drama has taught me that ..." and then we discuss a major theme **relevant to task**.

Theme 1: Race

Othello has become a play which can be dominated by readings that centralise race and racial tension. But, as mentioned before, Othello's actual race is hard to determine. The word "Moor" and even the word "black" do not have specific and fixed definitions for Shakespeare and his contemporary audience. Some uses of the word even just mean 'dark haired', swarthy or Mediterranean in origin. It is a general term which shifts, especially in the absence of much ethnic diversity.

But, certainly, for many modern audiences, the play has now got a deep interplay with race. Almost all adaptions have Othello played by actors who are people of colour or black. This means that it is almost impossible to see the play now without that clear racial dimension highlighted within the play. The presentation of Othello as a black man – or a person of colour – has become an integral part of the play.

Also, Brabantio's sheer opposition to Othello (a respected general) and Desdemona's marriage doesn't make sense unless Othello is demonstrably racially different to the cultural norms of the play and of the time. This is backed up by many of the racial stereotypes and epithets that are used through the play. So, we can be certain that Shakespeare intended this to be a central theme within the play itself. It may not be possible to specifically pinpoint exactly what Shakespeare meant by "Moor" or "black", but we can be sure that racial difference was at the forefront of his mind when creating the character.

The play itself as a piece of theatre also has a long history of racial controversy, especially when viewed through a modern lens. Specifically, this is in the area of white actors using make-up (or even soot) to blacken their skin and hair to play Othello. This, of course, has many connecting features to the historical use of 'black face' and/or minstrel shows. This was a practice that persisted in the theatre as Othello is considered one of the great tragic characters of Shakespeare and, therefore, many actors wished to play him.

Othello's 'blackness' was also, for a contemporary Shakespearean audience, a visual signal for a moral and spiritual darkness. This blackness for an Elizabethan audience had many negative connotations, such as violence, that Shakespeare is using to build tension within the play. This is highlighted when Othello is accused of witchcraft, a crime associated with Satanism and moral degeneracy. This reveals the inherent racism of the period and is (hopefully) something that must be explained to a modern audience watching the play.

This racial difference is highlighted by Shakespeare a number of times, especially contrasted with Desdemona's whiteness. Desdemona's purity is often tied up with her whiteness and then contrasted with Othello, creating a racially charged space. This is exploited by Iago, for example, to anger Brabantio in suggestive sexual language.

In fact, much of Othello's power resides in both how he is different from the racial stereotypes held about him– and how he seems to meet them. Othello is well-spoken, caring, and gentle towards Desdemona. He is also a skilled politician and tactician, rising to a high rank in Venetian society and earning the respect of that society. Yet, notice he has earned that power through violence (being a soldier) and, by the end, meets many of the negative stereotypes held about people of colour by the other characters on stage – out of control, angry, etc.

The lack of ethnic diversity – and Othello's race – are also a primary motivating factor for his manipulations at the hands of Iago. Othello is presented very much as isolated and lonely on stage, often criticised and stereotyped by others. This process of **othering** Othello creates an emotionally vulnerable man who is willing to believe the worst assumptions placed upon him. For example, Othello has been conditioned to believe his racial difference means that he is less attractive and, as such, leads to his belief that Desdemona would seek out a white lover. Othello internalises the prejudice he faces, and Iago manipulates this.

Race also plays a factor in explaining Iago's motivations, with racism being a factor in his desire to destroy Othello.

Theme 2: Jealousy

Jealousy is a driving but destructive force within the play. Iago experiences jealousy with Emilia, to the extent that Emilia says that it is part of the nature of all men to experience it. Iago is also jealous of Cassio and his promotion, a basic reason for his actions within the play. Interestingly, Iago expresses jealousy towards Othello for supposedly having sex with Emilia. Iago has no real evidence of this but even the possibility causes Iago to dislike Othello – this parallels the jealousy that he will create with Othello. So, jealousy can be seen as a core component of Iago's personality, something that he understands well and, so, something he finds it easy to create. Iago understands his own emotional make-up and understands how to weaponise it against Othello to cause the maximum destruction.

But the jealousy that Iago deliberately creates within Othello borders on obsessive and controls all of Othello's thoughts and actions. This differs from Iago's seemingly 'weak' jealousy of Cassio and Othello. So, what powers this jealousy? Well, Iago has noticed Othello's tendency to over-react and his fragile sense of self and uses these to drive Othello's jealous over the edge into madness. But it is a slow descent to this place that Othello experiences, carefully controlled and manipulated and encouraged by Iago. Jealousy totally destroys Othello's ability to reason, to see clearly and to trust appropriately - Othello only trust those ideas that reinforce his own prejudices and jealousy. Yet, this jealousy is very unstable and evaporates very quickly once Desdemona is cleared, showing its lack of substance.

Shakespeare, therefore, is presenting the danger of jealousy as a force in the human nature. He shows us how it can be exploited and how it is a feeling not to be trusted as its foundations are not true. He shows us that it is self-destructive, as represented by Othello's suicide at the end as a form of self-punishment. Shakespeare also interestingly presents jealousy as a particularly masculine trait, one not displayed by the female characters of the play to any great extent. They are not free of it but are not as defined by it as the male characters.

Theme 3: Love

Love presents an interesting dichotomy within this play. It overcomes very large problems, for example the difference in age, race and rank between Othello and Desdemona. It allows Othello to find a place in Venetian society, breaking down barriers that seem impossible to an audience. But love is destroyed or suffocated within this play by seemingly small problems, like a misplaced handkerchief. It is **mercurial** and changeable in its application and its place. It also

Shakespeare, therefore, seems to be showing how love is a positive force, one to be admired, but not necessarily depending upon. The foundations of love are easily assailable and easily undercut by jealousy, anger, and mistrust.

Theme 4: Deception and Trust

Othello is a frustrating character for audiences in part because he steadfastly trusts Iago. His trust is so fully misplaced and absent where it should be – Othello seems not to trust Desdemona at all, nor Cassio. Othello is also deceived by the person he trusts, and thinks he is being deceived (when he is not) by the people he should trust. For Othello, deception and trust seem inverted, or negatives of themselves: they are operating in the wrong places.

This inability to put his trust in the correct people – and to see when he is being deceived – makes Othello easy to trick, impulsive, and naïve. This is only made worse by the fact that he seems to get angry when those he considers liars or disloyal (such as Desdemona) protest their assured innocence. Othello only wants to hear what reinforces his own beliefs – this is why he trusts Iago, who is telling him what he already believes.

Shakespeare, therefore, is showing us the power of our own self-deception and how far it can cripple us. He is also showing us how fickle the human capacity to trust is, and how much we are driven by our own prejudice and self-delusion.

Theme 5: Military identity

Othello is first and foremost a soldier. This shapes both his sense of self and how he interacts with the world. His love for Desdemona is received with a sense of threat by Venetian society, but his prowess as a soldier and general is not questioned – in fact, it is celebrated. It is by being useful, productive and necessary on the battlefield that he earns his place in Venetian society.

This has shaped his thinking so much that, in fact, Othello considers love and his relationship with Desdemona in terms of a war to be won. This is emphasised by the fact that it is his war stories that initiated their relationship and is reflected in the fact that Desdemona enters a fortress on Cyprus in the second half of the play. It seems inevitable that the play ends in violence and with death as these are the 'currency' that soldiers and Othello has dealt in since the very beginning.

It is interesting to note that the play shows a shift in Othello. He begins the play by giving up his military identity to try and embrace his identity as a husband. Yet, when Iago questions Othello's manhood and virility (coupled with a declining need for Othello's war skills when the storm sinks the Turkish ships) he goes through an 'identity crisis' and tries to revert to the violence of being a war hero to find a sense of stability. He feels emasculated by Desdemona and his answer to this situation as a general is to eliminate her.

Shakespeare is interested in the military man. Figures such as Othello (generals, survivors of war, etc) are common ideas that he returns to. For a modern audience, there is a sense in which we could see Shakespeare trying to show the truth of war and how it destabilises the sense of self – a modern audience would call this Post-Traumatic Stress Disorder. Could this be the cause of Othello's emotional issues, including his fit?

Shakespeare is showing us a particular vision of manhood and holding it up for critique – and seems to be showing the audience that the military identity is, in some ways, lacking.

21

Theme 6: Isolation

Othello's otherness and race create a societal isolation for him which he seeks to remedy through military success to win respect from Venetian society. He is also looking for emotional support by finding love. Yet both these situations only highlight his isolation (Venetian society never quite accepts Othello, and Desdemona's extreme whiteness highlights his blackness). Othello's attempt to find acceptance exacerbate his isolation.

The largest chunk of the play also has the narrative setting of a fort in Cyprus which is not under threat, isolated form the rest of Venice. The characters are enclosed within walls, and the isolation of this group allows negative energies and emotions to run rampant through them, like a virus.

Physical isolation/distance is also used by Iago to create discord. He breaks ties between characters while also keeping himself distant to maintain his deceptions. There are many examples of Iago 'getting people' on their own to manipulate, and characters who are unattached are ostracised by the group (Roderigo, Cassio). Isolation is an indicator of weakness.

Shakespeare, therefore, is showing the audience the danger associated with isolation and loneliness, to emphasise the need for connects. He also presents self-isolation as a route to self-destruction rather than self-preservation.

Theme 7: Justice and revenge

Othello's actions are motivated by his own desire for justice for his wife's supposed transgressions. There would have been legal recourse if she had been cheating, but Othello's revenge is based upon his belief that he owns/controls her body and decides when she lives/dies. This interestingly parallels Brabantio's desire for justice from the beginning of the play for Othello's 'stealing' of his possession – his daughter.

Justice is presented tangled with revenge and is controlled by men – with women being objects of justice.

Main quotations
Some of the big quotes and analysis

This is a play that is packed full of 'quotes' that you could learn and analyse. There is no real way – or real need – to cover every single quotation. I have chosen what, to me, seem the most important or the most generally useable in a critical response.

Since you are probably thinking of writing an essay, the quotes are arranged chronologically from beginning to end. This allows you to choose quotes from the beginning, middle and end of the play – exam boards usually wants to see this. Any good essay will have **coverage** of the whole text, not just one part.

Each quote is also labelled with what **tasks** it will be useful for, for example what themes it discusses or what character it reveals. This will allow you to start thinking not just about analysis of quotes, but also how they might be used in order to answer a question in essay format.

Much of the analysis you will find here is 'commonly accepted' (i.e. most people would agree that this is what these lines mean or why they were written) but there is always room for your own ideas or differing interpretations.

You may have studied one of these quotations in your classroom and your teacher may have taught you something different – even the opposite – but the beauty of Shakespeare lies in the complexity ... there's room for multiple answers!

Act 1

"Tush! Never tell me"

Roderigo, Act 1 Scene 1

The play begins ironically with Roderigo telling Iago to "never tell" him, an action which is proved true at the end when Iago refuses to speak or explain his actions. The withholding of information, of not speaking and not speaking the truth, are important elements established in this moment.

The short syllable words, the use of the exclamation mark, and the use of the expletive ("Tush!") create interest within the audience for the events that are about to occur. The use of the expletive and the exclamation mark ("Tush!") are strong and have mild connotations of violence and frustration.

Tasks: Iago; dramatic irony.

"I know my price. I am worth no worse a place"

Iago, Act 1 Scene 1

Iago describes his dislike of Cassio: Iago feels that he is "worth" the promotion that Cassio achieved ("no worse a place"). The use of "price/worth" create a sense of the financial and transactional: Iago feels he has 'bought' the promotion with his loyalty and it has been stolen from him by Cassio.

In fact, Iago blames the corrupt Venetian society and thinks that Cassio only earned his promotion because he is a nobleman's son. There is an element of class within this moment as Iago is considered lower class and feels he should have "no worse a place" (i.e. be equal to Cassio) but he has been passed over. This is made more humiliating for Iago as Cassio has not had much (or really any) experience on the battlefield. Iago does not feel that Cassio has 'paid his dues' to use a financial phrase.

Both of these are elements that drive Iago's jealousy of Cassio and dislike of Othello.

Tasks: Iago; class; jealousy.

"I follow him to serve my turn upon him"

Iago, Act 1 Scene 1

Iago makes no secret to Roderigo (or the audience) of his intentions or his personality. He is very clear that he is a villain and wishes to do Othello harm ("serve my turn upon him"). The phrase "follow him" has connotations of back-stabbing while "serve" is ironic here because Iago appears to "serve" and be loyal, but "serve" in this context means to hurt. The word "upon" is also interesting as it has connotations of falling and striking, like Iago is planning to hurt him with a weapon.

Tasks: Iago; duplicitousness; jealousy; anger.

"I am not what I am"

Iago, Act 1 Scene 1

The repetition of the pronoun "I" shows his selfish nature, he only considers himself. Iago also ironically parodies God, whose names is 'I am who I am'. This makes Iago a Satan-like figure.

The irony in this sentence is that Iago is telling Roderigo the truth (that Iago is dangerous and not what he seems) but Roderigo still trusts him, not realising that Iago will also betray him - that Iago is also lying to him to get what he wants.

Tasks: Iago; duplicitousness.

"the thicklips"

Roderigo, Act 1 Scene 1

Roderigo describes Othello here. Mentions of "Moor" earlier in the scene made it clear to the audience that Othello is non-white, but this phrase shows Roderigo's disdain and racism.

The use of the definite article "the" shows the audience that Roderigo only defines Othello by his blackness, that he others him and destroys his right to exist by reducing him to just the racial stereotype of "thicklips".

Tasks: Roderigo; racism.

"an old black ram is tupping your white ewe"
Iago, Act 1 Scene 1

Iago and Roderigo go to Brabantio's window – Desdemona's father – and call up to him. They call out "thieves" to rouse him and imply that he has been robbed (meaning Desdemona).

Iago uses a negative sexual image. In this case Othello is the "black ram", Desdemona is the "white ewe", and "tupping" is sexual intercourse or rape. This entire image is laced with racism – and deliberately so as Iago wishes to anger Brabantio.

Notice that "tupping" is Iago reducing Othello and Desdemona's love to a sexual component. Certainly, at the start, Othello loves Desdemona dearly, but this is seen as unimportant. Secondly, the inter-racial relationship between the two characters is turned into something bestial, inhumane, and to be found disgusting.

This is further highlighted by the equating of Othello with a "ram", an animal. Othello is being denied his humanity. The "ram" is also associated with the devil and evil, with a "black ram" being one of the ways that the Devil could appear on Earth in Shakespeare's audience's mind. Othello is being associated with evil and the Devil, as he is later by Brabantio who accuses him of witchcraft. The "ram" is also associated with sexual appetites and being out of control (also a stereotype of black men) and so the racism is further layered.

Iago also further emphasises this situation by bringing to the fore Desdemona's whiteness – "white ewe". Iago wishes to build the image and contrast of "black" and "white" to anger Brabantio. Where "black ram" dehumanises Othello, "white" has associations of purity and innocence. The "white ewe" was also a costly creature so showing importance and worth, hence why it is important to be protected.

Yet, ultimately, Desdemona is reduced to property and an animal in this sentence. Although she is an 'important' animal to Brabantio, she and Othello still occupy a lower status in the power hierarchy of the play (although she is above Othello).

Tasks: Iago; Desdemona; Othello; racism; jealousy.

"your daughter and the Moor are now making the beast with two backs."

Iago, Act 1 Scene 1

One of Iago's most famous lines, a metaphor which became (for a long time) a common image for having sex: "making the beast with two backs". Desdemona's virginity was an absolute requirement and her husband would be picked by her father to uphold the family's position. If this is true, Desdemona has committed both an illegal action (fornication) but also a betrayal.

The metaphor of "beast" implies that Desdemona and Othello's lovemaking is grotesque, animalistic, and somehow inhuman. It creates an image of almost magical awfulness, invoking the idea of the Devil and the "ram" from earlier. Iago is being both blunt (almost vulgar in his mention of sex to anger Brabantio) but also subtle (hints of witchcraft and the devil).

Iago hammers home his point through the use of the possessive pronoun "your" to emphasise that Brabantio is having something stolen, while also implying Othello's violation of Desdemona is also, somehow, a violation of Brabantio and his position. The word "daughter" also brings to the forefront her youth and the word "Moor" emphasises the racist overtones of the situation, further angering Brabantio.

Tasks: Iago; racism; manipulation; Brabantio; sexuality.

"Thou art a villain"

Brabantio, Act 1 Scene 1

Brabantio recognised Roderigo, who often comes to plead to marry Desdemona – but doesn't recognise Iago who refuses to reveal himself. This is symbolic of Iago's role throughout the play: he hides and doesn't reveal his true self. Yet, despite not knowing who Iago is (or perhaps because he can't see him and so isn't fooled by appearances), Brabantio is the only person to call Iago a "villain" at the start and states it rather plainly.

Tasks: Brabantio; Iago; duplicitousness.

"She wish'd she had not heard it, yet she wish'd that heaven had made her such a man"

Othello, Act 1 Scene 3

Othello describes wooing Desdemona by telling her (and her father) stories of his personal and military history. They are so full of terrible events that she "wish'd she had not heard it" because of the pity and sympathy that they evoke. It is interesting that Othello – who often says that he is not well-spoken like other Venetian gentleman – wins over Desdemona's love through his storytelling. It is a mark of his intelligence.

Unlike Iago, who associates Othello's blackness with evil and the Devil, Desdemona associates Othello's race with goodness and "heaven". She also gives him humanity and identity by referring to him as a "man" and not an animal like others. Desdemona's capacity to see beyond racism is admirable.

Tasks: Othello; Desdemona; racism; love.

"My noble father, I do perceive here a divided duty"

Desdemona, Act 1 Scene 3

Desdemona immediately tells the truth to her father – she has married Othello and, as such, ha a "divided duty" between her family loyalty and that to her husband.

Desdemona does not reject her role as a daughter and member of Brabantio's family, seen by her complimentary "noble" and her use of "father". She has not forgotten her role and position and all that Brabantio has done for her – in fact, she lists "life and education" as reasons to love him and owe him "duty".

Yet the sharp d-sounds in the alliteration of "divided duty" emphasise the sharp, cutting remark that she is making – her honest has cut through this situation created by Iago and dissipated the tension and possible violence. The word "divided" shows us that she no longer 'belongs' just to Brabantio, but love moves her to have loyalty not to Othello.

Tasks: Othello; Desdemona; love.

"my ancient: a man he is of honest and trust: to his conveyance I assign my wife"

Desdemona, Act 1 Scene 3

Othello is sent to Cyprus to deal with a Turkish invasion. The Duke suggest Desdemona go back to her father's house, but Othello, Desdemona and Brabantio reject that idea. They settle on Desdemona going with Othello in a separate ship – this is Desdemona's idea as she wishes to be close to Othello.

In the above line, Othello entrusts Desdemona to Iago ("my ancient") for him to get her safely to Cyprus. Othello's blind spot for Iago is clear from the very beginning, calling him "honest" and someone to "trust". He, in fact, trusts Iago with the most precious thing in his life: "my wife".

Tasks: Othello; Desdemona; Iago; duplicitousness; love.

"Look to her, Moor, if thou hast eyes to see: She has deceived her father, and may thee."

Brabantio, Act 1 Scene 3

Brabantio's racism persists: "Moor". The use of the capitalisation is not uncommon as a referring title but also highlights that Othello is defined by his race. Brabantio also questions Othello's judgement ("if thou hast eyes to see") which also questions his ability to command and his station/masculinity. It is interesting that Othello, in fact, does not have "eyes to see" – for example, his trust of Iago and his belief in men over his wife.

This sentence by Brabantio is also one of many that set up the idea of Desdemona's falsehood which are build up by Iago, creating the tension and anger with Othello. There is some truth in Brabantio's line (Desdemona did keep her marriage to Othello secret) but this was done for Othello's own good as Brabantio would never have allowed the marriage. Yet Desdemona's deception of Brabantio leads Othello to believe she would deceive him to have an affair with Cassio.

Tasks: Othello; Desdemona; manipulation; duplicitousness.

Act 2

"O my soul's joy! If after every tempest come such calms, may the winds blow till they have waken'd death!"

Othello, Act 2 Scene 1

Othello arrives last on the island of Cyprus and sees Desdemona. The ships sailed through a terrible storm (that destroyed the Turkish fleet) and so Othello was scared that Desdemona have died and so is full of "joy" to see her alive. He goes so far as to say that she is part of his "soul", showing his love and affection.

The "tempest" that they have come through is a metaphor for the trials and tribulations that they will go through once they have reached the island. It could also be interpreted as God/fate working against Iago, attempting to keep Othello and Desdemona away from the trouble of the island. It could also be said that the "tempest" is, in fact a metaphor for Iago's lies surrounding the "calm" (Desdemona).

Othello states that the "calm" after this storm was worth the trouble (i.e. seeing Desdemona) and that he would do it and face "death". This is ironic considering the fact that he has come through this "tempest" only to kill Desdemona.

Tasks: Othello; love; fate; setting.

"the knave is handsome, young, and hath all those requisites in him that folly and green minds look after"

Iago, Act 2 Scene 1

Iago convinces Roderigo that once Desdemona will fall in love with Cassio ("handsome, young") after she is done with Othello. This is Iago's manipulations to kill and punish Cassio, using Roderigo like a weapon. Notice that Iago then uses the same trick against Othello. Iago seems to practice on a small scale (Roderigo, Brabantio) before turning the same manipulations and weapons on Othello, once he has perfected them.

Tasks: Iago; duplicitousness.

"Make the Moor thank me, love me and reward me for making him egregiously an ass."

Iago, Act 2 Scene 1

Here we see Iago think about reality in doubles or layers – there is the outward appearance of loyalty ("thank me, love me and reward me") and the inward truth of reality that only Iago can see ("making him egregiously an ass"). Iago derives power from manipulating others, which he does without thought and so easily, but also from being the only one within the centre of the storm who knows the truth of events – for being the only one who can see the truth clearly.

Once again Iago's inner racism comes out: he takes away Othello's name and reduces him to a title ("the Moor") that foregrounds his race; and, once again, equates Othello to an animal, this time an "ass".

It is also interesting to know that **rule of three** used by Iago: "thank me, love me and reward me". It contains the repetition of "me", which is Iago showing his self-centred nature. He puts himself at the centre of the sentence, as he feels the centre of reality, and repeats "me" to highlight his own importance. The last item in a **list** is usually the most important so it is worth noting that Iago starts with "thank" but ends with "reward" – financial and social gain is important to Iago. Yes, he enjoys hurting others, but he also intends to gain from this 'game'.

Tasks: Iago; racism; manipulation; duplicitousness.

"I learned it in England, where, indeed, they are most potent in potting"

Iago, Act 2 Scene 3

Iago gets Cassio drunk to embarrass him and Iago claims to have learned to drink in England. Shakespeare is joking as the audience in The Globe Theatre would be drinking. This audience address breaks the fourth wall rather: it is not a soliloquy.

Tasks: Shakespeare; theatre craft.

"I fear the trust Othello puts him in. On some odd time of his infirmity, will shake this island."

Iago, Act 2 Scene 3

Iago claims the drunken state of Cassio – who doesn't drink at all! – is a sign of his alcoholism. Iago is constantly sowing the seeds of discord within Othello's men, creating mistrust and misrepresentation wherever he goes. His plan was to get Cassio and Roderigo to fight but seems unable to stop himself to improvising other lines in the process (i.e. Cassio is an alcoholic). Is it a sign of Iago's quick mind in the situation, or is it sign of a pathological need to lie (one of the markers of a sociopath)?

Notice, once again, Iago's ironic statement: "I fear the trust Othello puts him in". It is Iago that Othello should, but does not, and it is Cassio he should trust, who ends up not trusting. Iago's power is to reverse situations so that they end up almost sitting in the opposite position to what they should.

Tasks: Iago; Cassio; Othello; duplicitousness.

"Cry within: 'Help! help!' Re-enter CASSIO, driving in RODERIGO"

Stage direction, Act 2 Scene 3

Roderigo arrives and follows a drunk Cassio off-stage to provoke him into a fight. Cassio won't remember the events and be convinced her started it (which ruins his reputation) and the other men think that Cassio is an alcoholic/not in control.

Cassio's anger is apparent from the phrase "driving" which shows that he is holding his sword, and the "cry" and "Help!" show that Roderigo is in danger. Roderigo is probably faking it a little in order to convince the other men on stage of Cassio's villainy, but Cassio is an adept soldier so it is possible that Roderigo could be losing this fight to drunken Cassio.

Cassio's drunken state causes the stage to descend into a general brawl amongst the men there.

Tasks: Cassio; stage craft; manipulations.

"if I once stir, or do but lift this arm, the best of you shall sink in my rebuke"

Othello, Act 2 Scene 3

Othello arrives and Iago helps him to break up the brawl – this makes Iago look calm and level-headed therefore building up Othello's trust in him for later.

This is one of the first signs of Othello's lack of self-control around situations which is a character failing for later with Desdemona. The phrase "if I once stir" is a metaphor for him holding himself back. Othello means if that he starts to fight and hurt the men then he will do real violence ("sink in my rebuke"). Othello would probably be clenching his fist ("lift this arm") to emphasise the point. In fact, Othello uses nautical metaphors to describe the level of violence that he would inflict, comparing himself to a cannon that would "sink" a ship.

This emphasises Othello's role as a solider, but in a small manner plays into the racial stereotype of the anger, lack of self-control and violence of a black man.

Tasks: Othello; self-control; racism; violence.

"I know, Iago, thy honesty and love doth mince this matter, making it light to Cassio. Cassio, I love thee but never more be officer of mine"

Othello, Act 2 Scene 3

The first stage of Iago's plan is a success: Cassio is demoted ("never more be an officer of mine"). Othello still shows loyalty to Cassio ("I love thee") but his men were brawling in the streets of the city Othello had come to protect – someone must be punished and it is Othello's duty to ensure that happens.

Notice that Iago's plan also raises his status ("honesty/love") and, in fact, Othello assumes that Iago's version of events is protecting Cassio out of loyalty ("making it light to Cassio"). Iago walks away from this first situation as true and loyal.

Tasks: Othello; Cassio; Iago; manipulations.

"Reputation, reputation, reputation! O, I have lost my reputation! I have lost the immortal part of myself, and what remains is bestial. My reputation, Iago, my reputation!"

Cassio, Act 2 Scene 3

Cassio sobers up after Othello's arrival but remembers little. The repetition of "reputation", the rule of three and the exclamations all emphasise the importance to Cassio. It is an important currency in Venetian high society, impossible to repair. Cassio compares harming his reputation to a deadly wound.

Cassio, in fact, equates his reputation to his soul ("the immortal part of myself"). He means his reputation was the purest and best part of himself, but his reputation as a soldier was also his route to immortality and remembrance after death due to great deeds. Having lost Othello's trust, Cassio has lost his place in the history books and his place in Venetian society.

Cassio's reaction to losing this is a little **hyperbolic** (exaggerated) and claims that all that is left is "bestial". Cassio feels sub-human. Notice the language Cassio is using about himself (he is like an animal) and how similar it is to language used about Othello. Even though Othello (in Act 1 and 2) has an impeccable reputation, Cassio's race and noble birth still give him advantages over Othello even in Cassio's weakened state.

Tasks: Cassio; reputation; duplicitousness.

"I'll pour this pestilence into his ear, that she repeals him for her body's lust"

Iago, Act 2 Scene 3

Iago convinces Cassio to get Desdemona to intercede with Othello, but Iago will convince Othello this is because they are having an affair ("pour this ... into his ear"). Iago compares his lies to "pestilence": a corrupting disease and almost like a witch, a bringer of disease. Notice his misogyny ("her body's lust") and degradation of Desdemona – Iago uses all societal negatives.

Tasks: Iago; manipulation; duplicitousness.

Act 3

"Ha! I like not that."

Iago, Act 3, Scene 3

Iago and Othello arrive on stage as Cassio is leaving after talking to Desdemona and Emilia. Iago has been waiting for this moment, a moment to suggest that there is something going on between Cassio and Desdemona.

The exclamation of "Ha!" is ironic because Iago is using it catch Othello's attention and to suggest that he and Othello have 'caught' Cassio and Desdemona at something they shouldn't be. But it is also an expression of his own happiness that something that he has hoped for is coming so easily to him.

The non-specific "that" is also interesting as Iago does not make it clear what he is talking about. He knows that Othello's jealousy will 'fill in the gaps' without needing to be specific. Iago is playing a careful and slow game, but one he is winning. He hammers home this suggestion in the next few lines by saying that Cassio "steals away so guilty-like".

Tasks: Iago; manipulation; duplicitousness.

"But I do love thee! and when I love thee not, chaos is come again."

Othello, Act 3, Scene 3

Othello agrees to let Cassio to come to see him after much badgering by Desdemona. As she leaves him and Iago, Othello muses on how much he is in "love" with her. The exclamation shows the depth and strength of this feeling.

Ironically, he discusses "when I love thee not" and what would happen: "chaos is come". This is exactly what happens at the end when Othello's love is destroyed. Yet notice the conjunction use of "when" and the present tense verb of "is" – they imply that Othello can already see/predict falling out of "love". It is fated.

Tasks: Iago; manipulation; duplicitousness.

"Is he not honest?"

Othello, Act 3, Scene 3

Iago gets Othello to question Cassio's motives. Othello's confusion can is seen in the use of a question but the negative construction (i.e. "not honest" rather than "liar") shows that Othello hasn't quite decided yet. Cassio still has the potential to be an "honest" man, but this has been placed into doubt.

Othello is asking this of Iago and its ironic for Othello to be asking the most dishonest person in the play for "honest" advice.

Tasks: Othello; Cassio; Iago; manipulation.

"I know thou'rt full of love and honesty, and weigh'st thy words before thou givest them breath, therefore these stops of thine fright me the more"

Othello, Act 3, Scene 3

Othello asks Iago a series of question which Iago refuses to answer ("these stops of thine"). This is a complex verbal trick that Iago is playing to draw Othello towards conclusions without Iago saying anything. It engages Othello and interests him – in fact, it allows the idea of Desdemona's infidelity to take a deep root in Othello's psyche – without Iago needing to do very much at all. Othello is leading himself down the path Iago wants him to go. Othello is filling in the blank spaces that Iago is leaving but this is a deliberate part of his manipulations – they are silences with meaning. A modern term for this would be 'gaslighting'.

This is a development of Iago's tactics, which depend so highly on his skills with language and manipulation. It shows his depth of understanding of both Othello specifically but human nature generally. Othello sees Iago as "full of love and honesty" and speaks carefully ("weigh'st thy words") and so these silences Othello takes only for bad news – news Iago makes him wait to here, creating tension and engagement in Othello and the audience.

Tasks: Othello; Iago; manipulations; Cassio.

"Men should be what they seem."
Iago, Act 3, Scene 3

Iago is speaking to Othello, telling him that Cassio "seems" honest and so "should" be an honest man. The use of the words "should/seem" though are unstable and immediately introduce doubt, therefore implying that Cassio is not what he "seems" and is not honest. Iago is still leading Othello gently into doubt.

Notice that Iago is doing something very subtle here: he is deliberately disconnecting appearance ("seem") from inner character ("should be"). In doing this, Iago is implying Cassio is dishonest while, in fact, implying that Cassio's appearance of honesty is proof of his dishonest nature! Iago does the same thing to Othello regarding Desdemona: he gets Othello to believe that the more Desdemona tells the truth, the more she is lying.

This is the first step in Othello being unable to distinguish truth from lie and reality from constructed falsity. This is the basis for much of the tragedy that will occur at the end of the play when Othello no longer has the ability to trust his love and affection for Desdemona because his belief in her honesty is so corrupted.

Iago also diminishes something naïve and innocent in Othello – "should" is a modal verb about hope, optimism and possibility. Othello believes in the best versions of people, who they "should" be. Iago takes this away from him, making Othello suspicious and full of doubt about the emotions of other people and, in fact, even doubting his own instincts and emotions.

Iago is also being rather brazen and bold here because he is looking Othello in the eye and telling Othello that men are not "what they seem" – that you can "seem" honest and not be – while this is exactly what Iago is doing in that exact moment to Othello. When you read the play, there are many moments where Iago skates close to warning Othello about himself. This is part of the joy of the game that Iago is playing: that he is almost telling Othello not to trust him over and over but Othello is too controlled and manipulated to realise that he is being told.

Tasks: Iago; Othello; manipulation; duplicitousness.

> *"O, beware, my lord, of jealousy; it is the green-eyed monster which doth mock the meat it feeds on"*

> *Iago, Act 3, Scene 3*

Iago has carefully constructed Othello's "jealousy" and then gives him a very fake warning about "jealousy" being a "monster". Iago is the first person to use the word within the play – he is giving this 'advice' in order to put the idea of being jealous of Cassio into Othello's mind – and is only manipulating Othello further.

Iago describes "jealousy" as the "green-eyed monster". This is a common metaphor which Shakespeare probably didn't invent but he certainly was the first writer to commit it to paper so is often called the 'inventor'. The colour "green" for a modern audience is associated with money, greed and being jealous of another's wealth or possessions. But this is not where the phrase comes from. It is most likely associated with sickness (much like the phrase for illness: 'green around the gills') and unripe fruit, which can cause stomach pain and illness. "Jealousy" is therefore a "monster" which causes us to go "green" and, like a sickness, eats away at us and causes us pain.

The "monster" element is fairly straightforward, but in this case the "monster ... doth mock the meat it feeds on". In this case, "meat" is the human that "jealousy" is consuming and to "mock" is to create pain as it eats away at us.

There is also a second image here of a tick or parasite: the "monster" is like a tick that "feeds" on doubt but the existence of "jealousy" in us only creates more and more doubts ("mock the meat") and so the monster gets larger and larger as it creates its own food. This is called an **entropic cycle**: a circular state of being that destroys everything due to its negativity. We cannot escape "jealousy" as it creates doubt to feeds itself, so growing.

Finally, the ultimate irony, is that Iago means the exact opposite of what he is saying: he wants Othello to become the "green-eyed monster". He is actively trying to make Othello into it ... and succeeds in doing so. By the end, Othello is a "monster" who kills.

Tasks: Iago; Othello; jealousy; manipulation.

"I speak not yet of proof. Look to your wife; observe her well with Cassio"

Iago, Act 3, Scene 3

Othello demands "proof" from Iago, who withholds it ("I speak not yet of proof"). This is because Iago doesn't have any proof, and also because he is aware that Othello's jealousy and anxiety needs to grow more in order to create the "monster".

Iago performs a neat verbal trick here – he presents Desdemona's very existence as somehow evidence: "look/observe". Iago presents Othello with the idea that just watching Desdemona will present him with the evidence that he needs. He also degrades her by refusing to name her ("wife/her") and so beings to strip of her identity, making it easier for Othello to associate her with wrongdoing.

This trick is particularly neat because Othello will be seeing evidence where there is none – and Iago doesn't even need to do anything! This further separates Othello's observable reality from truth, weaving a web of lies and mis-seeing around him.

This is then hammered home when Iago reminds Othello that Desdemona lied to her father (evidence that she is deceitful) and tells Othello that if Desdemona tries to get Cassio forgiven then that would be suspicious ("if your lady strains his entertainment") and evidence of their affair.

Tasks: Iago; Othello; jealousy; manipulation.

"I am glad I have found this napkin: This was her first remembrance from the Moor."

Emilia, Act 3, Scene 3

Othello suffers a headache and Desdemona tries to dab at his forehead. He pushes her off and she drops the "napkin"/handkerchief. This prop becomes central to Iago's plan once Emilia gives it to him – this is the piece of "proof" that Othello had demanded. Iago turns it into evidence of an affair.

Tasks: Iago; manipulation; theatre craft.

"Villain, be sure thou prove my love a whore, be sure of it; give me the ocular proof"

Othello, Act 3, Scene 3

Othello, in a short space of time, goes from doubting Iago and believing in Desdemona to calling her a "whore" and demanding "ocular proof". Shakespeare is doing this to move the play on (it is rather long!) but also to show the effects of jealousy upon our mind and souls, how quickly corrupting they are. This is the "monster" described by Iago or the effect of the "pestilence" or "poison" of doubt as Iago also calls it. It destroys love.

Even his language has changed which, in places was soft and complex – it now has become sharp, militaristic, pragmatic and a tad violent. This shift in language is representative in the shift in his personality and mindset.

This is one of the few places in the first Acts of the play that Othello directly identifies and sees Othello as a "villain" and someone who causes him pain, But he is so consumed by jealousy and doubt about Desdemona that he doesn't examine that instinct and, instead, focuses on "proof".

Tasks: Iago; Othello; manipulation; jealousy

"I think my wife be honest and think she is not; I think that thou art just and think thou art not."

Othello, Act 3, Scene 3

Othello's doubt is balanced on a knife edge, so much so that he speaks in balanced but contradictory statements. He is unable to trust her but unable to push aside his doubts – and the same is truth of his emotions towards Iago. This can be seen in the contrast between "art/art not" – direct opposites.

It is interesting to note that Othello uses the phrase "I think" implying that jealousy/doubt are infections of the mind not heart, and that Othello is almost existing in two realties at once and is unable to find which one is 'real'. Iago created that doubt.

Tasks: Othello; manipulation; jealousy.

"Even so my bloody thoughts, with violent pace, shall ne'er look back, ne'er ebb to humble love, till that a capable and wide revenge swallow them up"

Othello, Act 3, Scene 3

Iago mentions that Cassio has Desdemona's handkerchief (which, of course, he does not) the "ocular proof" that Othello demanded earlier. Notice Othello has yet to see this "proof" or ask for an explanation from Desdemona, but he is already discussing "bloody thoughts" (i.e. killing her). He has descended into his darkest thoughts quickly ("violent pace"). There is a sense in which Othello is acting before his love overwhelms him and he changes his mind, but it could also be part of the racist characterisation that the black man is so prone to violence.

His language has become dark and fierce ("bloody/violent") and also unstoppable ("pace/ne'er look back"). He balances "love" with "revenge", as if Desdemona has earned her death by making Othello love her and then betraying him. If Desdemona had committed adultery, then this was a crime that was punishable by law. But Othello doesn't not think along those lines - he wants "revenge" and not punishment.

It is possible that Othello is reacting in this manner because he is a soldier and used to being "violent". He is also a very masculine character and being **cuckolded** (i.e. being cheated on and not knowing) was a huge embarrassment to a man's masculinity, something which a character like Othello could not bear. Desdemona also represented Othello's access to high Venetian society despite his race and so her betrayal with Cassio (which is of course false) represents his loss of place – especially as Desdemona would appear to be choosing a white man over him.

Notice that this "revenge" that Othello is discussing is total and destructive, like a black hole ("swallow them up"). It is also interesting that Othello does not spare Cassio as the pronoun is plural: "them". Cassio will also be punished in this scenario. Othello wasn't just betrayed (he believes) by his wife, but also by a close friend and a subordinate in his own army.

Tasks: Othello; manipulation; jealousy.

"I think the sun where he was born drew all such humours from him"

Desdemona, Act 3, Scene 4

Desdemona is looking for the lost handkerchief and Emilia asks if Othello is jealous. Desdemona denies it ("drew all such humours from him") and implies that he is above or better than such emotions, which the audience know he is not.

Desdemona's reference to "the sun where he was born" is a coy reference to Othello's race and otherness but, rather than being a negative, she seems to imply that it has made him better than Venetian men who are prone to jealousy. What others see as a negative within him, she views as a positive.

The word "drew" in reference to jealousy is also ironic here because poison is drawn out – and Iago earlier referred to the doubts he was creating in Othello as poison. Desdemona and Iago's language are oppositional to each other as they see different sides to Othello: positive and negative, giving and taking poison. This opposition of Iago and Desdemona is representative of the battle for Othello's soul.

Tasks: Desdemona; Othello; love; racism.

"The handkerchief!"

Othello, Act 3, Scene 4

Othello arrives in a strange mood, claiming that the handkerchief was woven by a witch and it contains a magical power. Desdemona begins to panic, realising how important it is and how Othello will react to losing it. Yet she still tries to get him to speak to Cassio, but Othello responds with a demand to see "the handkerchief!" and repeats the same line four times.

The exclamation mark shows his growing anger and mistrust, while the shortness of the sentence shows the shortness of his patience. Her not having it on her seems to be proof of her affair.; her lack of it is becoming a symbol of a lack of love.

Tasks: Desdemona; Othello; love; manipulations.

"They are all but stomachs, and we all but food; to eat us hungerly, and when they are full, they belch us"

Emilia, Act 3, Scene 4

This is Emilia's pronouncement on men and on love. She describes a very different kind of relationship than Desdemona is experiencing, who is freshly married. Emilia's version of love is related to appetite and the body, almost a function of the body rather than an emotion. It is also related to the women's world (dinner and food) unlike Othello's discussions of love, which are related to war and conquering as he is a solider.

In Emilia's theory women are passive ("food") and used by men. There is a sense of a women's role is to be consumed by a man, much as food is prepared purely to be eaten. She also describes men as something monstrous, consuming and destructive ("stomachs") yet balances this by making them comical and disgusting ("belch").

She equates the loss of men's love as poor table manners – something we discover as we get to know someone.

Tasks: Emilia; love; relationships.

"My lord is not my lord"

Desdemona, Act 4, Scene 4

When Cassio asks for further help, Desdemona tries to tell him that she may be of no use as Othello is an odd humour and not acting him like him ("is not my lord"). Notice that she still gives him the respect of her husband ("lord") and the sentence is laced with confusion more than anything else, a sense of not understanding what is happening.

It is also interesting that Iago's gift of creating two opposing realities through doubt in Othello has now spread to Desdemona – the jealousy created by Iago has created a reality in which Desdemona describe Othello as "my lord" and "not my lord" due to his irrational behaviour. This is almost a paradox.

Tasks: Desdemona; Othello; manipulation; jealousy.

"But jealous souls will not be answer'd so; they are not ever jealous for the cause, but jealous for they are jealous: 'tis a monster begot upon itself, born on itself"

Emilia, Act 3, Scene 4

Emilia's description of jealous matches the earlier one provided by Iago, showing how closely linked and similar husband and wife are. In fact, they use exactly the same vocabulary to describe jealousy: "monster". This could be due to Iago's own jealous nature (remember Iago is worried that Emilia has had sex with Othello), and Emilia could be describing Iago here.

Notice Emilia has a lovely description of that **entropic cycle** described earlier: "begot upon itself, born on itself". This implies that jealousy breeds within itself (like a self-pollinating weed or a virus) and replicates endlessly. It is a "pestilence" that cannot be stopped by normal means. This description turns jealousy from a mere emotion into something mythic and powerful.

Emilia also uses a **tautology** to describe jealousy: "jealous for they are jealous". Tautologies are explanations that employ repetition to explain and are syntactically locked (i.e. contain no outside information). Emilia uses it to show the self-replication of jealousy, its confusing nature, its irrationality, and that it has no reason or core for existence.

Tasks: Emilia; jealousy.

"Giving her DESDEMONA's handkerchief"

Stage direction, Act 3, Scene 4

Bianca (Cassio's lover) arrives briefly and Cassio hands her the handkerchief. This is the first time the audience has seen it since Emilia handed it over and they wonder how Cassio got it. Bianca assumes Cassio has a new lover, but Cassio describes finding it on his bedroom floor. Iago's plan here seems to be a little haphazard, implying that he is becoming more reckless. Fate has worked in his favour here, but it was a risk that Iago took.

Tasks: Cassio; stage craft; Iago; manipulation.

Act 4

"Lie with her! lie on her! We say lie on her, when they belie her. Lie with her! that's fulsome. --Handkerchief--confessions--handkerchief!—To confess, and be hanged for his labour;-- first, to be hanged, and then to confess"

Othello, Act 4, Scene 1

Iago claims that Cassio has been bragging about having sex with Desdemona and leverages the "handkerchief" as proof. Othello struggles to accept what he is hearing which causes a fracturing in his love and his psyche. Despite saying repeatedly that he isn't as eloquent as white Venetians due to being a man of colour, Othello has been sophisticated in his speech up until now. But now his language is broken, nonsensical and almost riddle-like. This fracturing is represented in his broken and incoherent speech patterns, which are shown in the dialogue as short sentences and the use of dashes. This violent and short language also represents Othello's temper while the collapse of his language represents the collapse of his love and psyche.

Interestingly, madness was often considered a curse of witchcraft in Jacobean England and, in some sense, Iago is showing some of these signs of witchcraft – certainly his effect on Othello is extreme, like a spell, and Iago has referenced the Devil and witchcraft a number of times.

Othello uses repetition in this quotation, especially of "lie". He uses it to mean sexual intercourse between Desdemona and Cassi, but also that they have lied to him. He is levelling a double accusation at her (adulterer and liar) in the **pun**. The use of the exclamation marks also shows his confusion/anger at this version of Desdemona being constructed as she is so different from the 'real' Desdemona he loves.

Other repetitions ("handkerchief/confess") represent Othello's inability to think about anything else, specifically his concern for proof. But he is no longer wondering if it is true; he is now concerned only with finding evidence to prove his jealousy.

Tasks: Othello; madness; jealousy; doubles.

45

"My lord is fall'n into an epilepsy: this is his second fit; he had one yesterday."

Iago, Act 4, Scene 1

Othello is provoked a kind of "fit" which is interestingly called a "trance" in the stage directions. Iago's lies have done this and is another way in which Iago's power seems to be aligning with a kind of witchcraft or inhumane power.

Iago then describes this as the "second fit" to Cassio, trying to imply the instability of Othello – and, obviously, setting up the believability of his murder of Desdemona. This is similar to how Iago laid the groundwork for Cassio being an alcoholic when he had a chance. Iago repeats similar manipulations and tricks across several characters within the play.

Tasks: Iago; manipulation; Othello.

"A horned man's a monster and a beast"

Othello, Act 4, Scene 1

Othello describes himself as a "horned man", a reference to the Jacobean idea of a **cuckold**. This is a man whose wife is openly cheating on him and he is deceived by her. This is metaphorically represented as a man with stag antlers, which is humiliating to the man, both personally and socially.

In this case, Othello takes his perceived state of being a cuckold and transfers it into being a "beast" and a "monster", a devil with horns not a cuckold. Othello seems to be degrading himself (implying that Desdemona has transformed him into a "beast"). It is possible that Othello is trying to dehumanise himself to justify the anger and violence he is about to commit.

Othello is taking something passive (a cuckold) and creating a violent active state (a demon) – specifically a state of being with violent power, a power reminiscent of his earlier status and masculine power as a solider. Othello would rather be a murdering "beast" than mocked as a cuckold.

Tasks: Othello; violence; Desdemona.

"Do but encave yourself, and mark the fleers, the gibes, and notable scorns, that dwell in every region of his face"

Iago, Act 4, Scene 1

Iago encourages Othello to hide and listen to Cassio and Iago talking. Iago will have Cassio talk about a sexual encounter with Bianca but has made Othello believe it is about Desdemona. It is a rather simplistic trick, but Othello is in such a desperate and fractured state that he believes and falls for it.

Notice that Iago is, once again, presenting non-specific items to Othello as definitive proof of infidelity, for example "notable scorns". Can facial expressions really show cheating? Of course not, but Iago has Othello convinced that they can.

Iago also succeeds because this is a very clear example of a tactic, he uses a lot: isolation of individuals. He literally hides Othello away on his own, cutting him off from lines of communication (with Cassio or Desdemona) that can interfere with his plan. Iago succeeds in part by isolating and disconnecting groups and relationships and using that isolation to his advantage.

Tasks: Iago; manipulation; Othello; isolation.

"[Advancing] How shall I murder him, Iago?"

Othello, Act 4, Scene 1

Othello's immediate reaction is violent and deadly ("murder"). This is also reflected in Othello's physicality on stage as he is "advancing" in the stage direction, which gives a sense of power and movement to it. It seems rather personal, as seen in the personal pronouns in the sentence ("I [...] him"). This is very clearly a revenge scenario and not for justice.

Notice that Othello turns immediately to Iago. There is a sense in which Othello is unconsciously aware that Iago is in control, seen in the use of questions towards Iago. This is a reflection of Othello's soldier identity – he expects and follows orders.

Tasks: Iago; manipulation; Othello; identity.

"Do it not with poison, strangle her in her bed, even the bed she hath contaminated"

Iago, Act 4, Scene 1

Othello initially wishes to "poison" Desdemona, a common way to murder someone in Venice, but worries that Desdemona's good nature and beauty will prevent him from carrying it out. Iago encourages him to "strangle her" – a much more painful and violent death – and that Othello must do it tonight. Iago knows that Othello's pain will be further compounded by the traumatising act of strangling his wife – Iago is planning to maximise the pain that Othello is going to feel.

Notice that Iago once again uses the language of disease ("contaminated") and corruption, which is ironic as it is Iago's presence that is the corrupting force. The "bed" in this case is a direct reference to the supposed sexual intercourse between Cassio and Desdemona, which Iago makes to keep Othello's anger burning. But the "bed" is also a metaphor for Desdemona and Othello's love and relationship which has been "contaminated". Once again, it has been – but not by Cassio. It has been destroyed by Iago's lies.

Tasks: Iago; manipulation; Othello; jealousy.

"[Striking her] Devil!"

Othello, Act 4, Scene 1

A letter arrives calling Othello home but promoting Cassio to the role of Governor of Cyprus. Desdemona says she is glad of his as she loves Cassio and Othello strikes her.

The stage direction of "striking" is active, violent and powerful. It represents his resentment and power over her. It is also a word associated with animals (vipers and snakes) and weapons (swords) showing Othello's nature as a "beast" and soldier.

The short sentence and exclamation of "devil" emphasise his belief that she is evil and beyond redemption.

Tasks: Othello; jealousy; violence

"What doth your speech import? I understand a fury in your words. But not the words."

Desdemona, Act 4, Scene 2

Othello interrogates Emilia and Desdemona about the affair without directly saying what he believes. Othello's indirect accusations leave Desdemona confused ("What doth your speech import?") and Desdemona recognises a double state in Othello here: "fury in your words/But not the words". This anger that is fuelling Othello is recognised by Desdemona ("fury") but she doesn't know why ("not the words").

The dramatic shift in Othello is confusing to Desdemona. Remember, the audience have watched Othello being worked over by Iago, but Desdemona has found her husband totally changed. She has no explanation for this. She senses she is being blamed for something but isn't sure what it is. And Othello effectively never allows Desdemona the ability to refute or answer the accusations because he never tells her what they are. He is worried that she will be able to convince him not to kill her and, in effect, Othello has already decided.

He is also 'pretending' he doesn't know about the affair to hold power over Desdemona, much as Iago holds power over other characters. Othello's manipulations reflect the manipulations that he has endured from Iago. He is attempting to isolate Desdemona (literally by asking Emilia to stand outside) but also to put her in an emotionally vulnerable state where he can verbally and emotionally attack her, a light form of punishment for her betrayal before he takes her life.

This also represents another moment where a lack of emotional control overwhelms Othello and interrupts his ability to effectively communicate. He is speaking and his emotion is clear ("fury") but he cannot communicate the reason ("not the words"). Iago's whirlwind of lies (interestingly a kind of "fury also") has fractured Othello's reasoning mind too much for anything other than emotional reactions to situations.

Tasks: Othello; jealousy; violence; manipulations.

"Was this fair paper, this most goodly book, made to write 'whore' upon?"

Othello, Act 4, Scene 2

Othello compares Desdemona to a book, once again emphasising her whiteness ("fair paper") and contrasting it with blackness and sin (i.e. black ink) being written upon it ("whore").

It is interesting that Othello assigns an active verb ("to write") to her action – it is not just her betrayal that hurts him, but it is the active choice that he perceives Desdemona made.

It is also a further metaphor for an inside/outside dichotomy. Just as the "goodly book" contains the negative word "whore", so Othello is trying to understand how Desdemona's beauty, whiteness and outward goodness can containing a soul so black, dark and full of sin. Of course, this is dichotomy doesn't exist (Desdemona is the good person she appears) and Othello's confusing dichotomy that is driving him to madness and murder is purely a fiction of Iago.

Tasks: Othello; jealousy; appearances; manipulations.

"The Moor's abused by some most villanous knave, some base notorious knave, some scurvy fellow"

Emilia, Act 4, Scene 2

Othello's accusations towards Desdemona are overheard by Emilia, who then brings in Iago. Desdemona is devastated as this accusation ruins her reputation, allowing for the possibility of her execution for adultery. Emilia is outraged on her behalf as seen by her language ("abused/villainous/notorious/scurvy"). Emilia is well-aware that these charges are false.

Interestingly Emilia correctly identifies that there is someone manipulating Othello ("some scurvy fellow") but fails to realise it is her husband, the person she is talking to. The **dramatic irony** in this situation is of Emilia insulting the "knave" to his face without knowing it is him.

Tasks: Othello; jealousy; appearances; manipulations.

"I will make myself known to Desdemona: if she will return me my jewels, I will give over my suit and repent my unlawful solicitation; if not, assure yourself I will seek satisfaction of you."

Roderigo, Act 4, Scene 2

Roderigo is angry at Iago, who has been taking Roderigo's money ("jewels") and claiming to be giving it to Desdemona on his behalf to woo her. He has, of course, been stealing the money. Desdemona knows nothing of this, but Iago has been claiming that Desdemona is in love with Roderigo.

This represents the beginning of the unravelling of Iago's plans. It is the first time that someone has had enough of Iago's lies and lack of results. In fact, Roderigo threatens Iago ("I will seek satisfaction") which could be a legal threat (to sue) or it could be a personal threat (to kill).

Iago manages to convince him to kill Cassio as a way to Desdemona's heart, but only just. Iago's web of lies and deceit is beginning to unravel around him.

Tasks: Iago; manipulations.

"If I do die before thee prithee, shroud me in one of those same sheets."

Desdemona, Act 4, Scene 3

Desdemona asks Emilia to lay out her wedding "sheets" onto her bed. This is an attempt to remind Othello of their love and they are something that Desdemona is proud of and loves dearly and, so, asks to be buried in them ("shroud me") if she was to "die". This represents the importance of her love for Othello.

The irony of this statement (as the audience is aware) is that Othello intends to strange her and she will "die" soon. This prop represents the mixing of love ("sheets") with death, love and despair which is the end result of Iago's manipulations.

Tasks: Othello; Desdemona; love; dramatic irony.

Act 5

"Now, whether he kill Cassio, or Cassio him, or each do kill the other, every way makes my gain"

Iago, Act 5, Scene 1

Iago is encouraging Roderigo to fight Cassio. Iago believes he has set up a situation which is win-win ("every way makes my gain") for him. It is representative of the power of Iago's manipulations that two characters with no quarrel are fighting and that either outcome benefits Iago. The use of the list and repetition of the word "or" show the thoughtfulness and conniving nature of Iago: he has thought through the multiple scenarios and how they work for his benefit or his "gain". There is a plan in this chaos.

The use of "gain" shows us that Iago's motivation is still partially to do with financial and socially improvement. Shakespeare does tilt Iago as 'bad for bad's sake' in many places, but here Iago still seems to be trying to convince either himself or the audience that part of his reasoning is "gain".

Tasks: Iago; manipulation; duplicitousness.

"IAGO from behind wounds CASSIO in the leg, and exits."

Stage Direction, Act 5, Scene 1

Iago takes direct action to "wound" his enemy, Cassio. This is the first outright attack he takes, and notice that he does this from "behind", representative of his secretive and manipulative nature. He's not a coward (he is a solider) so is capable of fighting but chooses from "behind". Why? Well, it is symbolic of his other attacks., also from "behind" in order to inflict damage.

It must also be noted that the wound is on the "leg" – it is low, unexpected and hinders forward movement. This makes Cassio's suffering greater, inflicts permanent damage, and prevents him from chasing Iago. It is also the area that a viper or snake would strike, which Iago has been compared to a number of times.

Tasks: Iago; manipulation; duplicitousness; attack.

"O murderous slave! O villain! [Stabs RODERIGO]"
Iago + Stage Direction, Act 5, Scene 1

Cassio and Roderigo cry murder and various people come to help. The setting is night and dark so no-one can see/find each other which leads to confusion, isolation and a lack of understanding about events.

This kind of chaos which Iago thrives in.

In the darkness, unseen by others, Iago calls out "villain!" as if looking for the person who has stabbed Cassio. This is Iago signalling that he is a good person and helping. His voice (Iago's greatest weapon) is being used in order to continue the lie that he is a good and loyal soldier and man.

Yet, at exactly the same time, he has secretly found Roderigo and the audience see him "stab" Roderigo to keep him silent and to prevent being found out. There is a mismatch between what Iago is saying and what Iago is doing and the only people who can 'see' this are the audience, creating a layer of **dramatic irony** to what is happening on stage.

The word "stab" is violent, destructive and evil. It is a quick escalation of Iago's evil from merely wounding Cassio moments ago. We can see Iago is taking more and more direct action in order to secure his place. There are some who argue that Iago is only acting like this in a form of desperation (to keep everything secret) but it is possible it is a form of confidence because everything is going his way. He is now over-confident.

Shakespeare is also making a comment on the magic and trickery of the stage itself. It is, of course, not dark on the stage. The actors are only pretending in order to create the scene. We are being told the stage is dark by

The lies of Iago only work because those listening are willing to believe, just as the lies of the stage only work if the audience allow them. Iago, the master manipulator, is a dark and negative version of Shakespeare himself: someone who controls reality through language and makes everyone 'see' what he wants.

Tasks: Iago; manipulation; violence; stage craft.

"Kill me to-morrow: let me live to-night!"
Desdemona, Act 5, Scene 2

Othello comes to Desdemona's chamber and makes it clear he will kill her for having an affair. Desdemona asks for Cassio to be brought to prove her innocence (notice that her word alone is not good enough) but Othello tells her that Cassio is dead.

In Desdemona's fear she begs for her life – her desperation and fear of Othello can be seen in the exclamation mark. These represent the drama and violence of this moment of the play, just as he is about to strangle her.

Desdemona begs for even a little more time – a day, night, and even a half hour. She is hoping to put him off to earn more time for herself to prove her truth which is, in fact, exactly what she needed! In a few moments. the whole situation will unravel, and her honesty proved but Othello has acted too hastily, driven by jealousy.

Tasks: Othello; Desdemona; love; jealousy; violence.

"The noise was here. Ha! no more moving? Still as the grave. Shall she come in? were't good?- I think she stirs again:-no"
Othello, Act 5, Scene 2

Othello kills Desdemona ("Still as the grave") and Emilia knocks on the door to speak to him ("Shall she come in?"). The disjointed sentences, the various sentences lengths, the use of exclamations combined with questions and the presence of dashes all represent his broken and fractured speech patterns, showing his fear and out of control mental state.

Notice the contrasting of non-movement ("still as the grave") which represents death/his crime with his desire for movement ("I think she stirs again") and her to be alive. We, the audience, are unsure if he has successfully killed her – and, in fact, it turns out that she is still partially clinging on but will die.

In essence, another double: she is both alive and dead here.

Tasks: Othello; Desdemona; love; jealousy; violence.

"Nobody; I myself. Farewell. Commend me to my kind lord: O, farewell!"

Desdemona, Act 5, Scene 2

With her dying breath, Desdemona is asked who killed her and she refuses to name Othello. Desdemona, at first, blames "nobody" and then, interestingly, takes the blame for her own death upon herself ("I myself") despite having done nothing wrong. She loves and is trying to protect Othello. This can also be seen in the use of the word "kind" to describe him. She reinforces this self-blame by using self-referential pronouns ("myself/me/my") to drive home this idea that she has done this to herself, which is patently untrue.

Her repetition of "farewell" is meant to be a verbal indicator to the audience that the character is dying. Remember, it would be hard for much of the audience at the time to fully see the stage and so these verbal cues are needed to understand events.

Desdemona uses a **pun** or double meaning in her final line: "commend me" refers both to 'pray for me' and 'send my love to' and "my kind lord" is a reference to both God and Othello. She is asking to be prayed for by Emilia before she dies but also for Emilia to Othello that she loves him as her final words.

Tasks: Othello; Desdemona; love; jealousy; violence.

"the more angel she, and you the blacker devil!"

Emilia, Act 5, Scene 2

Othello admits to killing Desdemona and Emilia curses him. She calls him a "devil", implying that he is evil and full of sin. She also raises his race ("blacker") and highlights the difference between Othello and Desdemona by calling her an "angel", which has associations of purity and whiteness. Remember she is also surrounded by her wedding sheets (that would be white) and these may also look like angel's wings, highlighting the spiritual and physical differences between Othello and Desdemona.

Tasks: Othello; Desdemona; love; jealousy; contrast.

"O mistress, villany hath made mocks with love, my husband say that she was false!"

Emilia, Act 5, Scene 2

Othello raises Iago's name as proof of Desdemona's affair and Emilia is shocked, as seen in the exclamation mark above. In fact, Emilia repeats the words "my husband" four times in this small sentence, so deep is her disbelief and realisation of Iago's central role in the plot against Desdemona.

Emilia's language shows her fidelity to Desdemona ("O mistress"), her disgust at her husband ("villany") and her quick understanding of the situation ("hath made mocks with love/false"). Iago's plot unravels very quickly and notice what it takes: two characters to speak to each other. Iago's system of isolation and control collapses when characters communicate and interact, a fundamental weakness of his manipulations.

Tasks: Othello; Iago; Emilia; manipulations.

"Help! help, ho! help! The Moor hath kill'd my mistress! Murder! murder!"

Emilia, Act 5, Scene 2

Emilia cries for "help". Her distress can be seen in the short sentences and the use of exclamation marks. Her repetition of "murder" emphasises her distressed state and the violent act committed by Othello. Emilia's desperation and fear of Othello, that he may hurt her to keep his secret, is apparent in this moment and is reflected in her frantic sentences.

Once again Emilia sinks back into describing Othello not with his name but his race "Moor" and the definite article of "the", creating a title and removing his identity. Her narrative in this moment becomes less that a husband has killed his wife but is now that a black man ("Moor") has murdered a white woman ("my mistress"). She is revealing her racism in the moment and that, ultimately, his race matters more now than his motivation.

Tasks: Othello; Iago; Emilia; manipulations.

"[He runs at IAGO. IAGO, from behind, stabs EMILIA, and exit]"
Stage direction, Act 5, Scene 2

Iago and others arrive, and Emilia refuses Iago's instruction to go home and reveals that she found the "handkerchief" and that Desdemona was falsely accused. Iago attempts to stab her once t get her to be quiet, missed, and then "stabs EMILIA" in order to save himself from Othello and distract everyone and escape. It shows his heartless and self-serving nature that he would kill his own wife in order to escape proper justice.

Notice that, like earlier, he "stabs" but "from behind" and strikes unexpectedly. Like much of what Iago does, this is an escalation of a similar behaviour we have seen of him before (with Cassio).

Tasks: Iago; justice.

"O thou Othello, thou wert once so good, fall'n in the practise of a damned slave"
Lodovico, Act 5, Scene 2

Iago tries to run but is re-captured and Othello non-lethally stabs him. He deliberately makes it a non-lethal blow because he sees death as a release from proper justice. Othello confesses his crime and guilt openly, seeming genuinely sorry for his actions.

In the above quotation Othello is equated with Satan with an angel's fall from grace: "wert once so good" shows us that Othello had reputation, status and respect, which the past tense ("wert") tells us has now gone; he is referred to as "fall'n" which is what happens to angels when they lose their grace and become devils; and, finally, he is referred to as a "damned slave", someone with no hope or place. In this case "slave" is both a reference to Othello's race, but also to his future imprisonment which is assured due to his murder of Desdemona.

Othello was described as a "beast" and devil at the beginning, which is exactly what he has become. Now we have to question: how much of this is natural and how much is Iago's creation?

Tasks: Othello; race; Iago; manipulation.

"Demand me nothing: what you know, you know: from this time forth I never will speak word."

Iago, Act 5, Scene 2

Iago is questioned and this is his response: "I never will speak word". Iago's final power move is to refuse to speak, to refuse to explain to anyone his motivations. The audience are aware of a number of reasons, but many of the characters on the state do not understand why he did the things that he has. They do find a letter from Roderigo outlining (and they also say that they will torture Iago) so some explanations will be forthcoming.

But this is Iago's final manipulation and it is ironic that it is the opposite of his action throughout most of the play – Iago has used language and speaking to get what he wants, but in this moment his refusal to use language is what gives him power over others. Iago's silence is his final control over others.

This is reinforced by his use of the word "nothing", which is exactly what he is going to give them. This lack of knowledge is reinforced by the repetition of "what you know, you know" which is a circular statement, creating a kind of tautology that implies a lack of new knowledge or information.

Tasks: Iago; manipulation.

"when you shall these unlucky deeds relate, speak of me as I am; nothing extenuate, nor set down aught in malice"

Othello, Act 5, Scene 2

Othello speaks of himself in a vaguely past tense manner ("these unlucky deeds relate"), a verbal cue he plans to kill himself. He asks for fair judgement ("speak of me as I am"): he does not wish actions to be downplayed ("nothing extenuate") nor does he wish to be a devil ("nor set down aught in malice").

Notice it is the story/narrative (and, therefore, his reputation and how he is remembered) which Othello is concerned about. There is sense of trying to control history post his death.

Tasks: Othello; justice; manipulation; reputation.

"I kiss'd thee ere I kill'd thee: no way but this; killing myself, to die upon a kiss"

Othello, Act 5, Scene 2

Othello stabs himself ("killing myself") and addresses his final lines to the corpse of Desdemona, which is still lying on the bed on the stage. The stage now has two dead bodies (Desdemona, Emilia) and three wounded (Cassio, Iago and Othello). The number of deaths and woundings are clear visual signals to the audience that the play is ending, and it is a tragedy.

Othello, once again, speaks in doubles: "I kiss'd thee ere I kill'd thee". He means this literally, which is that he kissed Desdemona just before he strangled her. But, also, metaphorically, in that his love ("I kiss'd thee") was the cause of her death. If he had never met herm, and they had never fallen in love, then she would still be alive. His love was the cause of her death.

Notice that he does show anger towards Iago, but these final lines do not seem to blame Iago – Othello is very much taking the blame upon himself. Would Othello still have killed Desdemona without Iago's "poison" and "pestilence"? It seems unlikely to the audience, but Othello here seems to imply that it was almost always destined to happen due to his love.

There is also a sense of poetic justice for Othello in that his kiss brought her death and now he is dying and the last thing he will do is "die upon a kiss". The romantic and the tragic are here and now very much entangled. This has many striking similarities to *Romeo and Juliet*, which ends in a similar double-death of lovers.

Shakespeare cleverly highlights this mixing of love and death for the audience through the use of alliteration and repetition: "kiss'd/kill'd/killing/kiss". This k-sound and use of consonance links the words within the audience's ear (they sound similar so they must be linked together) to further bring them together. Their similar sound linguistically links them through the use of sound techniques. The repetitive plosive k-sound (harsh, strong) also relates to the hash nature of both love and death.

Tasks: Othello; love; destiny; violence; jealousy.

Writing an essay

Yeah, but how do I write an essay?

Okay, well, let's start with the fact that your teacher has probably taught you some structures already, and you've probably practised it since you were in your first years of senior and/or secondary education! You know how to write an essay – all that knowledge is tucked away in your brain somewhere.

But if you need a little reminder, here's some advice....

Task

The exam paper has a task on it. This is what is going to drive your essay. You should be referring to that task twice in every paragraph of your essay. We usually use the **key word from the task** in the first line and last line of each paragraph.

This is called 'topping and tailing' – it is at the top and tail of each paragraph. This lets the marker know that you are definitely answering the question/doing the task. This is guaranteed to up your mark.

Do not just write all the information that you know. Only write information that is relevant to an appropriate task. For example, if you decide to write about romantic love – why are you talking about Iago's character? You may know about it, but it probably isn't fully relevant! This loses marks.

Introductions

These are not explicitly in most mark schemes (although "structure" usually is and introductions are a point of structure), but they are expected by all markers. They allow the marker to understand the task, text and approach you are going to take. They set the scene, set up the essay, give the marker the low down, etc. An essay without an introduction just seems odd!

There are standard things introductions contain:

- **Title in inverted commas:** "Othello"
- **Full name of author:** William Shakespeare
- **Reference to task:** I am going to discuss ...
- **Some sort of summary:** This drama is about

Weaker introduction

Task: discuss a drama where there is major theme.

I am going to discuss "Othello" by William Shakespeare. I am going to talk about the major theme of jealousy that is present in this play. This play is about a black man and white woman who get married, but Iago breaks them apart using jealousy.

Better introduction

Task: discuss a drama where there is major theme.

William Shakespeare's "Othello" is a drama where the major them, and central concern, is the emotion of jealousy. Iago, the main antagonist in this drama, uses jealousy like a weapon against his commanding officer, Othello, and his new wife, Desdemona. Iago convinces Othello that his wife is having an affair and - coupled with racial tensions and careful manipulations - Iago manages to destabilise Othello's sense of self and love enough to almost force him to kill his new wife. Iago is an arch-villain who uses jealousy like a carefully targeted, heat-seeking missile to destroy Othello, and I will discuss how.

Analytical paragraphs

These are the paragraphs that make up the **body** of your essay. This is mostly what your marks are going to come from. You need to make sure you have a minimum of three – one from the start, one from the middle and one from the end. This shows coverage. You probably want to work **chronologically** (start to middle to end) rather than out of order.

You may have been taught an acronym (PEA, PEAR, PCQE, etc) for producing these. These systems do work. I am going to speak more generally, and you should see it's the same information I'm telling you – just different terminology.

The standard things included in analytical paragraphs:

- **A literary technique:** The writer uses a simile
- **Reference to the task:** This creates the theme
- **A quotation in " " marks**: "whore"
- **Knowledge of the drama**
- **Analysis of the quotation**

Weaker analytical paragraphs

Task: discuss a drama where here there is major theme.

Shakespeare uses imagery, "whore". This is from Act 1. This is what Othello thinks of Desdemona. This shows his jealousy.

Better analytical paragraphs

Task: discuss a drama where here there is major theme.

Shakespeare uses a negative insult, "whore". This is Act 3 Scene 3 where Othello goes from doubting Iago to victimising Desdemona. This good woman becomes "whore" – a word containing implications of liar, manipulator, duplicitousness; criminal and evil. This shows the effects of jealousy upon our mind and souls, how quickly corrupting jealousy is as a force and how careful we must be when it enters our minds and hearts.

Conclusions

Like, introductions, these are not explicitly in most mark schemes (again "structure" is and conclusions are a point of structure), and so are expected by markers. They summarise your ideas, round off your essay, give you a last chance to say anything to show a lesson that you have learned.

There are standard things conclusions contain:

- **Concluding phrase:** In conclusion,
- **Repeat in inverted commas:** "Romeo and Juliet"
- **Repeat full name of author:** William Shakespeare
- **Reference to task:** I have discussed …
- **Personal reaction:** I have learned …

Weaker conclusion

Task: discuss a drama where there is major theme.

In conclusion, I have discussed "Othello" by William Shakespeare. I have talked about the major theme of jealousy. This play shows us a jealous character and teaches us not to be like him – we need to avoid it at all costs.

Better conclusion

Task: discuss a drama where there is major theme.

In conclusion, William Shakespeare's "Othello" is a drama defined by the major theme of jealousy–the driving force of the narrative. It is jealousy that creates unfounded and unreal doubt, corrupting Desdemona's positive reputation. In fact, it is jealousy that distorts reality to take Desdemona's honesty and, in fact, make honesty proof that she is a liar. Finally, it is jealousy (the "green-eyed monster") which drives Othello into an act of murder. Shakespeare is clearly showing us the corrupting and consuming power of jealousy, and in the 'anti-hero' of Othello is showing us how susceptible even the best of us are to this force.

63

Disclaimer about the use of exemplars:

Exemplars are useful ways to 'see' what high end essays look like and understand what to sound like when you write your own. It can even be useful to try to memorise parts or ideas from an exemplar to write in your exam!

You fully have my permission to use these exemplars to *inform* your own work, and as revision/learning tools for an exam. That's what they were created for.

But **plagiarism** is never acceptable

This is trying to pass off an exemplar as piece of homework or claiming that you have written it when you did not. Especially when that work forms part of a grade awarded to you by a teacher.

Your teacher will know! Don't be a fool!

Exemplar Essay 1

Discuss a drama with a memorable character (Iago).

"Othello" by William Shakespeare is a drama which focuses on the tragedy of Othello, a black General of the Venetian army who marries a white noblewoman. Yet, through the manipulations of his "ancient" (a trusted commander), Iago, Othello is consumed by the "green-eyed monster" of jealousy and kills his wife due to false accusations of adultery. Othello may be the eponymous central character but this narrative pivots and turns on the actions of the memorable Iago, a manipulative villain of the highest calibre. He is not only memorable for his villainous acts, but also for his duplicitousness nature, his cunning and intelligence, and his verbal dexterity.

First, Shakespeare uses contrast to make Iago a memorable character, "I am not what I am". This is Act 1 Scene 1 where Iago is discussing openly his hatred for Othello. At this moment he seems primarily driven by jealousy of Othello's promotion of Cassio over Iago. The repetition of the pronoun "I" shows Iago's selfish nature and how he only considers himself. Iago also ironically parodies God, whose names is 'I am who I am'. It implies Iago's sense of his own power and strength which, although is hyperbolised in this section, is not inaccurate – Iago does go on to prove how much power he has over the others.

Iago's ability to weave lies and create stories is certainly formidable and, in this way, resembles a god of the play in the sense that he is a creator and destroyer. The inversion of 'I am who I am' into "I am not what I am" therefore links Iago linguistically to both God but also Satan, the opposing figure of God. There is a long history in English Literature of Satan-like figures who exercise power through language and convincing others (Marlowe's *Faustus* or Milton's *Paradise Lost*) and Iago is part of that continuum. One of the ways that Shakespeare establishes Iago here as memorable is the way that he speaks the truth about being a villain: he is open and honest about his villainy. And the irony in this sentence is that Iago is actually telling Roderigo the truth (that Iago is dangerous and not what he seems) but Roderigo still trusts him, not realising that Iago will also betray him - that Iago is also lying to him to get what he wants. Iago manages to layer truth and lie so closely together here that they are indistinguishable to the listener, creating a memorable character from the very beginning of the play.

Shakespeare further establishes this memorable character and his linguistic power through the use of innuendo and metaphor, "your daughter and the Moor are now making the beast with two backs." One of Iago's most famous lines in Act 1 Scene 1 said to Desdemona's father, a metaphor which became (for a long time) a common image for having sex: "making the beast with two backs". Desdemona's virginity was an absolute requirement and her husband would be picked by her father to uphold the family's position. If this is true, Desdemona has committed both an illegal action (fornication) but also a betrayal. The metaphor of "beast" implies that Desdemona and Othello's lovemaking is grotesque, animalistic, and somehow inhuman. It creates an image of almost magical awfulness, invoking the idea of the Devil and the "ram" from earlier. Iago is being both blunt (almost vulgar in his mention of sex to anger Brabantio) but also subtle (hints of witchcraft and the devil). Iago hammers home his point through the use of the possessive pronoun "your" to emphasise that Brabantio is having something stolen, while also implying Othello's violation of Desdemona is also, somehow, a violation of Brabantio and his position. The word "daughter" also brings to the forefront her youth and the word "Moor" emphasises the racist overtones of the situation, further angering Brabantio. All of this combines to create a linguistic weapon, almost a sledge-hammer, which Iago uses to attack Brabantio and through him Othello. Iago's linguistic trick here – one he will use again – is to attack Brabantio's love for his daughter, his masculinity, his innate racism, his innate sexism, and his reputation. The intellect and power over language Iago wields throughout this play cannot be denied – and neither can we deny the way that he manipulates others – and these combine to create a very memorable character.

A further way that Iago is made memorable by Shakespeare is through imagery and links to witchcraft, ""I'll pour this pestilence into his ear, that she repeals him for her body's lust". In Act 2 Scene 3 Iago describes how he will convince Othello of Desdemona's affair Iago compares his lies to "pestilence": a corrupting disease. It will not only destroy Othello's soul, but Iago seems already to be aware that, like a disease, it will end with the death of Othello. Notice Iago's misogyny ("her body's lust") and degradation of Desdemona – Iago feels no sorry over the mistreatment of Desdemona because he has no respect for her. In fact, the noun "body" and pronoun "her" seem to reduce Desdemona's identity to nothing, implying that Iago doesn't even really seem women as human beings. It is also interesting to note the finishing on the word "lust" which has some connotations of Iago's own "lust" and sexual desire for Desdemona, giving us a possible other reason for his destruction of Othello –jealousy for his beautiful wife. Finally, Iago has linguistically linked himself to the Devil and witchcraft a number of times in the play before this point. But here the link becomes more obvious. Witchcraft in the Jacobean era was a high crime as it meant an embracing of the devil and a rejection of God. It was a crime punishable by death. One of the powers of a witch was the ability to bring disease and "pestilence" and, so, Iago's use of this word has a weight and power behind it. He is not saying that he is a witch, but he is showing a self-awareness that his manipulative gifts are inhumane or unnatural in some way, almost superhuman, making him a memorable character.

Shakespeare develops the memorable character of Iago using word choice, "Men should be what they seem". In Act 3 Scene 3 Iago is speaking to Othello, telling him that Cassio "seems" honest and so "should" be an honest man. The use of the words "should/seem" though are unstable and immediately introduce doubt, therefore implying that Cassio is not what he "seems" and is not honest. Iago is still leading Othello gently into doubt. Notice that Iago is doing something very subtle here: he is deliberately disconnecting appearance ("seem") from inner character ("should be"). In doing this, Iago is implying Cassio is dishonest while, in fact, implying that Cassio's appearance of honesty is proof of his dishonest nature! Iago does the same thing to Othello regarding Desdemona: he gets Othello to believe that the more Desdemona tells the truth, the more she is lying. This is the first step in Othello being unable to distinguish truth from lie and reality from constructed falsity. This is the basis for much of the tragedy that will occur at the end of the play when Othello no longer has the ability to trust his love and affection for Desdemona because his belief in her honesty is so corrupted. Iago also diminishes something naïve and innocent in Othello – "should" is a modal verb about hope, optimism and possibility. Othello believes in the best versions of people, who they "should" be. Iago takes this away from him, making Othello suspicious and full of doubt about the emotions of other people and, in fact, even doubting his own instincts and emotions. Iago is also being rather brazen and bold here because he is looking Othello in the eye and telling Othello that men are not "what they seem" – that you can "seem" honest and not be – while this is exactly what Iago is doing in that exact moment to Othello. This is part of the joy of the game that Iago is playing: that he is almost telling Othello not to trust him over and over but Othello is too controlled and manipulated to realise that he is being told. This sheer level of devilish manipulation makes Iago memorable.

Another tactic that Shakespeare uses that makes Iago memorable is isolation, seen in the use of imagery in Act 4 Scene 2, "Do but encave yourself, and mark the fleers, the gibes, and notable scorns, that dwell in every region of his face". Iago is here encouraging Othello to hide and listen to Cassio and Iago talking. Iago will have Cassio talk about a sexual encounter with Bianca but has made Othello believe it is about Desdemona. It is a rather simplistic trick, but Othello is in such a desperate and fractured state that he believes and falls for it. Notice that Iago is, once again, presenting non-specific items to Othello as definitive proof of infidelity, for example "notable scorns". Can facial expressions really show cheating? Of course not, but Iago has Othello convinced that they can. Iago has detached reality (Cassio talking about Bianca) from fantasy (affair with Desdemona) and is creating a glamour and fake visual symbols around the lie ("notable scorns"). Iago also succeeds because this is a very clear example of a tactic which he uses a lot: isolation of individuals. He literally hides Othello away on his own, cutting him off from lines of communication (with Cassio or Desdemona) that can interfere with his plan. In fact, Iago even makes this isolation a virtue ("encave") that will reveal truth to Othello, when it brings only lies and misinformation. Iago succeeds in part by isolating and disconnecting groups and relationships and using that isolation to his advantage. For example, Iago understands that Othello feels racially isolated in society and uses this to create doubt in him about Desdemona's (how could a noble white woman love a "Moor"?) and, so, Iago repeatedly uses and shows a deep knowledge of isolation as a tool. This may stem from the way in which Iago presents himself as being outside and isolated from the group, but above them – like a puppet-master from the outside controlling everything. Iago takes a weakness in others (isolation) and turns it into a manipulative strength for himself. This a memorable and powerful trait of the character, one carefully crafted.

Finally, a powerful way that Shakespeare makes Iago memorable is from his final action in the play, seen in the use word choice: "Demand me nothing: what you know, you know: from this time forth I never will speak word." Iago in Act 5 Scene 2 is questioned about why he has committed these crimes, and this is his response: "I never will speak word". Iago's final power move is to refuse to speak, to refuse to explain to anyone his motivations. The audience are aware of a number of reasons, but many of the characters on the state do not understand why he did the things that he has. They do find a letter from Roderigo outlining some reasons (and they also say that they will torture Iago) so some explanations will be forthcoming, but this is Iago's final manipulation and it is ironic that it is the opposite of his action throughout most of the play – Iago has used language and speaking to get what he wants, but in this moment his refusal to use language is what gives him power over others. Iago's silence is his final control over others. This is reinforced by his use of the word "nothing", which is exactly what he is going to give them. This lack of knowledge is reinforced by the repetition of "what you know, you know" which is a circular statement, creating a kind of tautology that implies a lack of new knowledge or information. This final refusal to speak creates a memorable and powerful villain for the audience watching.

In conclusion, "Othello" by William Shakespeare is a drama which focuses on the tragedy of Othello, yet it is the manipulation and characterisation of Iago which generates the action of the play, creating a manipulative villain of the highest calibre. He is not only memorable for his villainous acts, but also for his duplicitousness nature, his cunning and intelligence, and his verbal dexterity. Iago's capture and punishment at the end of the play is a very clear message to the audience about the morality of Iago's decisions, while his constant linking to the Devil and witchcraft leave us in no doubt as to Iago's ultimate fate. Yet, it is be noted how attractive and seductive as a character Iago is. The audience do not exactly support him, but we are carried along with him and his manipulations to a certain extent, seduced by his villainy and power. This is what makes Iago such a memorable character and secures his place in the canon of English Literature alongside other great villains.

Exemplar Essay 2

Discuss a drama with an important theme (jealousy).

"Othello" by William Shakespeare is a drama which focuses on the tragedy of Othello, a black General of the Venetian army who marries a white noblewoman. Yet, through the manipulations of his "ancient" (a trusted commander), Iago, Othello is consumed by the "green-eyed monster" of jealousy and kills his wife due to false accusations of adultery. Othello may be the eponymous central character but this narrative pivots and turns on the actions of the memorable Iago, a villain of the highest calibre and the way in which jealousy is created, stoked and used as a weapon against Othello and the other characters within this play. Shakespeare very much presents jealousy as a consuming and destructive force which one must be careful of, a force which can lead a character into darkness and despair.

To begin, Shakespeare establishes jealousy as a weapon used by Iago through a metaphor, "an old black ram is tupping your white ewe". In Act 1 Scene Iago and Roderigo go to Brabantio's window – Desdemona's father – and call up to him. They call out "thieves" to rouse him and imply that he has been robbed (meaning Desdemona). The primary emotion Iago is evoking is a jealousy and possessiveness in Desdemona's father achieved using a negative sexual image. In this case Othello is the "black ram", Desdemona is the "white ewe", and "tupping" is sexual intercourse or rape. This entire image is laced with racism and deliberately so as Iago wishes to anger Brabantio. Notice that "tupping" is Iago reducing Othello and Desdemona's love to a sexual component and, ultimately, Desdemona's virginity is a possession of her father and family's and, so, in using this sexual imagery Iago hopes to provoke jealousy and possessiveness within her father for the loss of reputation and power that will come from this loss of her virginity. Iago also further emphasises this situation by bringing to the fore Desdemona's whiteness – "white ewe". Iago wishes to build the image and contrast of "black" and "white" to anger Brabantio. Where "black ram" dehumanises Othello, "white" has associations of purity and innocence. The "white ewe" was also a costly creature so showing importance and worth, hence why it is important to be protected. Yet, ultimately, Desdemona is reduced to property and an animal in this sentence. Although she is an 'important' animal to Brabantio, she and Othello still occupy a lower status in the power hierarchy of the play (although she is above Othello). Therefore, Iago is provoking fatherly and possessive jealousy in Brabantio to make him lose control and bring ruin to Othello – the same weapon and reasoning used by Iago later in the plan on others, which we will see.

Next, Shakespeare has Iago use this weapon against Othello, created using sentence structure and imagery in Act 3, Scene 3, "Ha! I like not that." Iago and Othello arrive on stage as Cassio after talking to Desdemona and Emilia. Iago has been waiting for this moment, a moment to suggest that there is something going on between Cassio and Desdemona. The exclamation of "Ha!" is ironic because Iago is using it catch Othello's attention and to suggest that he and Othello have 'caught' Cassio and Desdemona doing something they shouldn't be. This plosive non-word creates tension where there is none and is almost triumphal on Iago's part. It is an expression of his own happiness that something that he has hoped for is coming so easily to him. It is interesting here that Iago (a master of words) begins his plans not with words but animalistic sounds, non-words. He slowly builds up to complex words, sentences and ideas, like ensnaring Othello in an ever more complex web. The non-specific "that" is also interesting as Iago does not make it clear what he is talking about. He knows that Othello's jealousy will 'fill in the gaps' without needing to be specific. Iago is playing a careful and slow game, but one he is winning. He hammers home this suggestion in the next few lines by saying that Cassio "steals away so guilty-like". Overall, we can see how Iago is attempting to create and establish jealousy where there is none, creating a target for his weapon. It is done with subtlety and it is opportunistically created.

In fact, in Act 3 Scene, Shakespeare (through Iago) uses a metaphor to lay out his theory of jealousy, "O, beware, my lord, of jealousy; it is the green-eyed monster which doth mock the meat it feeds on". Iago has been carefully constructing Othello's "jealousy" and then here gives him a very fake warning about "jealousy" being a "monster". Iago is the first person to use the word within the play, but he is giving this 'advice' in order to put the idea of being jealous of Cassio into Othello's mind. It is only manipulating Othello further. Iago describes "jealousy" as the "green-eyed monster". This is a common metaphor which Shakespeare probably didn't invent but he certainly was the first writer to commit it to paper so is often called the 'inventor'. The colour "green" for a modern audience is associated with money, greed and being jealous of another's wealth or possessions. But this is not where the phrase comes from. It is most likely associated with sickness (much like the phrase for illness: 'green around the gills') and unripe fruit, which can cause stomach pain and illness. "Jealousy" is therefore a "monster" which causes us to go "green" and, like a sickness, eats away at us and causes us pain. The "monster" element is fairly straightforward, but in this case the "monster ... doth mock the meat it feeds on". In this case, "meat" is the human that "jealousy" is consuming and to "mock" is to create pain as it eats away at us. There is also a second image here of a tick or parasite: the "monster" is like a tick that "feeds" on doubt but the existence of "jealousy" in us only creates more and more doubts ("mock the meat") and so the monster gets larger and larger as it creates its own food. This is called an entropic cycle: a circular state of being that destroys everything due to its negativity. We cannot escape "jealousy" as it creates doubt to feeds itself, so growing. Finally, the ultimate irony, is that Iago means the exact opposite of what he is saying: he wants Othello to become the "green-eyed monster". He is actively trying to make Othello into it ... and succeeds in doing so. By the end, Othello is a "monster" who kills and is motivated purely by his jealousy, or "green-eyed". Therefore, jealousy is not a minor theme within this play but, in fact, a philosophical theory and a state of being Shakespeare is warning us of through its effect primarily on the character of Othello.

Shakespeare begins to show us the effect of jealousy on Othello in Act 4 Scene 4 through sentence structure and word choice as voiced by Desdemona, "What doth your speech import? I understand a fury in your words. But not the words." Othello interrogates Emilia and Desdemona about the affair without directly saying what he believes. Othello's indirect accusations leave Desdemona confused ("What doth your speech import?") and Desdemona recognises a double state in Othello here: "fury in your words/But not the words". This anger that is fuelling Othello is recognised by Desdemona ("fury") but she doesn't know why ("not the words"). Jealousy has twisted him into an unrecognisable shape and version of himself, one that Desdemona cannot comprehend. The dramatic shift in Othello is confusing to Desdemona. Remember, the audience have watched Othello being worked over by Iago, but Desdemona has found her husband totally changed. She has no explanation for this. She senses she is being blamed for something but isn't sure what it is. And Othello effectively never allows Desdemona the ability to refute or answer the accusations because he never tells her what they are. He is worried that she will be able to convince him not to kill her and, in effect, Othello has already decided. He is also 'pretending' he doesn't know about the affair to hold power over Desdemona, much as Iago holds power over other characters. Othello's manipulations reflect the manipulations that he has endured from Iago. He is attempting to isolate Desdemona (literally by asking Emilia to stand outside) but also to put her in an emotionally vulnerable state where he can verbally and emotionally attack her, a light form of punishment for her betrayal before he takes her life. This also represents another moment where a lack of emotional control and jealousy overwhelms Othello, interrupting effective communication. His emotion is clear ("fury") but he cannot communicate the reason ("not the words"). Iago's whirlwind of lies (interestingly a kind of "fury also") has fractured Othello's reasoning mind too much for anything other than emotional reactions to situations. Here we see that jealousy creates broken-states and isolation: it is a disharmonising emotion that only fractures.

Finally, Shakespeare explores the long term effect of jealousy through the imagery used by Othello in the closing of the play, "when you shall these unlucky deeds relate, speak of me as I am; nothing extenuate, nor set down aught in malice". In Act 5, Scene 2 Othello speaks of himself in a vaguely past tense manner ("these unlucky deeds relate"), a verbal cue he plans to kill himself. Yes, the most dramatic effect of jealousy within the play has been the death of Desdemona, but earlier the "green-eyed monster" was described as consuming itself and, so, this has come to pass as Othello plans to kill himself. Yet he asks for fair judgement ("speak of me as I am"): he does not wish actions to be downplayed ("nothing extenuate") nor does he wish to be a devil ("nor set down aught in malice"). He does not wish his memory to be too distorted through the lens of his final actions, implying that jealousy doesn't represent the totality of him (though it does represent the worst). Notice it is the story/narrative (and, therefore, his reputation and how he is remembered) which Othello is concerned about. There is sense of trying to control history post his death and not allow jealousy to corrupt him in the immortal sense.

In conclusion, "Othello" by William Shakespeare is a drama which focuses on the theme of jealousy, a central concern of the play. It is the driving force of the narrative, created by Iago and brought to living flesh in Othello. Yet Shakespeare is clearly setting up a warning to the audience about susceptibility to jealousy and the ease with which it can be created – and its consumptive, fracturing and destructive power. Beware the "green-eyed monster" indeed – it might be you!

Exemplar Essay 3

Discuss a drama with a relationship that drives the narrative (Othello/Iago)

"Othello" by William Shakespeare is a drama which focuses on the tragedy of Othello, a black General of the Venetian army who marries a white noblewoman. Yet, through the manipulations of his "ancient" (a trusted commander), Iago, Othello is consumed by the "green-eyed monster" of jealousy and kills his wife due to false accusations of adultery. Othello may be the eponymous central character but this narrative pivots and turns on the actions of the memorable Iago, a villain of the highest calibre. The relationship between these two male characters, Iago and Othello, defines the narrative and the outcome of the drama, creating a powerful message on the nature of misplaced trust and the manipulation of others.

First, Shakespeare uses metaphorical language to clearly define Iago's part in the relationship from Act 1 Scene 1, "I follow him to serve my turn upon him". Iago makes no secret to Roderigo (or the audience) of his intentions or his personality. He is very clear that he is a villain and wishes to do Othello harm ("serve my turn upon him"). The phrase "follow him" has connotations of back-stabbing and being behind in order to do Othello mischief, while "serve" is ironic here because Iago appears to "serve" and be loyal, but "serve" in this context means to hurt. The word "upon" is also interesting as it has connotations of falling and striking, like Iago is planning to hurt him with a weapon (in this case, the weapon being used will be jealousy). This all clearly defines Iago's part in the relationship between the two men and it creates dramatic irony throughout the play that we, the audience, are privy to the real nature of the relationship between Iago and Othello when Othello himself is not and is deceived by his seeming friend.

Next, Shakespeare defines Othello's part in the relationship between the two men in Act 2, "I know, Iago, thy honesty and love doth mince this matter, making it light to Cassio. Cassio, I love thee but never more be officer of mine". This is Othello in Act 2 Scene 3 when the first stage of Iago's plan is a success: Cassio is demoted ("never more be an officer of mine") after a brawl in the street caused by Iago. Othello still shows loyalty to Cassio ("I love thee") but his men were fighting in the streets of the city Othello had come to protect – someone must be punished and it is Othello's duty to ensure that happens. Notice that Iago's plan also raises his status ("honesty/love") in the eyes of Othello so we now have a strange tension where the actions designed to break the relationship (Iago's scheming) seem to be making their friendship stronger. It is also ironic that Othello assumes Iago is protecting Cassio out of loyalty ("making it light" i.e. making Cassio's crime seem less) when Iago feels no loyalty to anyone at all. Ultimately, the audience see the relationship between Iago and Othello here as very imbalanced with the cunning Iago seeming to manipulate and control Othello with Othello ironically grateful for this, unaware.

One of the way that this relationship drives the narrative can be seen in how Iago abuses this loyalty and trust in Act 3, as created by Shakespeare through word choice, "I know thou'rt full of love and honesty, and weigh'st thy words before thou givest them breath, therefore these stops of thine fright me the more" (Othello, Act 3, Scene 3). Othello asks Iago a series of question about Desdemona's supposed affair, which Iago refuses to answer ("these stops of thine"). This is a complex verbal trick that Iago is playing to draw Othello towards conclusions without

Iago saying anything. It engages Othello and interests him – in fact, it allows the idea of Desdemona's infidelity to take a deep root in Othello's psyche without Iago needing to do very much at all. Othello is leading himself down the path Iago wants him to go as Othello is filling in the blank spaces that Iago is leaving but this is a deliberate part of his manipulations – they are silences with meaning. Othello sees Iago as "full of love and honesty" and as someone who speaks carefully ("weigh'st thy words") and so these silences Othello takes only for bad news – news Iago makes him wait to here, creating tension and engagement in Othello and the audience. A modern term for this would be 'gaslighting' and shows how Iago abuses the relationship and trust that Othello has in him, knowing that Othello will assume the worst of his supposed friend's silences. This is a development of Iago's tactics, which up until now have depended so highly on his skills with language and manipulation. It shows his depth of understanding of both Othello specifically but human nature generally. It is, once again, ironic that Othello should know his friend both well and not at all: Othello is correct in that Iago "weigh'st … words" (i.e. thinks before speaks) but Othello is wrong in assuming Iago is like this to be honest. He is like this to think about how best to hurt Othello. This is just one moment of many where Iago exploits his understanding of Othello and the relationship between them.

Yet, Shakespeare emphasises the instability of this relationship through the use of inversion and repetition, "I think my wife be honest and think she is not; I think that thou art just and think thou art not." Othello's doubt is balanced on a knife edge, so much so that he speaks in balanced but contradictory statements. He is unable to trust Desdemona but unable to push aside his doubts – and the same is truth of his emotions towards Iago. This can be seen in the contrast between "art/art not" – direct opposites. It is interesting to note that Othello uses the phrase "I think" implying that jealousy/doubt are infections of the mind not heart, and that Othello is almost existing in two realties at once and is unable to find which one is 'real'. Iago created that doubt but is now also subject to that doubt – Othello feels a sense of doubt towards Iago's lies until he gives "proof".

Othello will no longer be led just by his trust and relationship with Iago. He now needs objective proof in order to choose a 'reality' to exist in and to know what to do next. Iago's verbal manipulations of their relationship are not enough.

Shakespeare has Iago provide this proof in Act 4 and develops the relationship between Iago and Othello further through the use of command and instruction, "Do but encave yourself, and mark the fleers, the gibes, and notable scorns, that dwell in every region of his face". Iago encourages Othello to hide and listen to Cassio and Iago talking. Iago will have Cassio talk about a sexual encounter with Bianca but has made Othello believe it is about Desdemona. It is a rather simplistic trick, but Othello is in such a desperate and fractured state that he believes and falls for it. Notice that Iago is, once again, presenting non-specific items to Othello as definitive proof of infidelity, for example "notable scorns". Can facial expressions really show cheating? Of course not, but Iago has Othello convinced that they can. Iago also succeeds because this is a very clear example of a tactic, he uses a lot: isolation of individuals. He literally hides Othello away on his own, cutting him off from lines of communication (with Cassio or Desdemona) that can interfere with his plan. Iago succeeds in part by isolating and disconnecting groups and relationships and using that isolation to his advantage. Iago is also using his own relationship, which Othello thinks is his only real relationship at this point, to exploit and isolate Othello, an already isolated member of society due to his race. Iago is isolating this already isolated individual, knowing this makes him easier to control and manipulate. This control can be seen very clearly in the above quotation in that Iago, the junior officer, is giving subtle commands to Othello now. He is literally moving him around the stage and placing him in areas, like a puppeteer. The supposed objective "proof" that Iago offers gives him more control over Othello, creating an even more manipulative but one-sided relationship.

Finally, in Act 5, the stage directions reveal the final resting place of this relationship that has driven the narrative of tis entire play, "[He runs at IAGO. IAGO, from behind, stabs

EMILIA, and exit]". Iago and others arrive to find that Othello has killed Desdemona, and Emilia refuses Iago's instruction to go home. She reveals that she found the "handkerchief" and that Desdemona was falsely accused. Iago's plans collapse almost immediately, and it is interesting to note how quickly Othello goes from complete trust of Iago to realising he has been duped. In fact, "he runs at Iago" shows that he trying to kill him – Othello goes from total loyalty to attempting to murder him almost instantly. The relationship between the two men collapses so quickly because it was never real, and Othello realises this quickly. The speed of collapse also seems to imply that Othello knew all along that Iago was being false since Othello was so quick to realise that Iago was manipulating him. In the end, even the lightest breath of truth being spoken by Emilia was all it took to collapse Iago and his hold/relationship over Othello.

In conclusion, "Othello" by William Shakespeare is a drama which has a power relationship: the controlling Iago's friendship and supposed love for his leader and general Othello. Shakespeare shows us the power that relationships have upon us, the ability that the loyalty and trust has to drive us forward. It is, in part, Othello's relationship with Iago which allows Iago to manipulate and control the other man so powerfully., These two characters orbit each other, their negative aspects so equally created (Iago's power to manipulate and Othello's susceptibility to manipulation) that they seem almost fated to exist parasitically together. This destroys any room or space for positive relationships, such as between Othello and Desdemona. So, therefore, Shakespeare seems to be offering a warning about many things in this play (jealous, revenge, justice) but there is a strong warning about choosing friends wisely and being careful about whom we allow to enter our lives.

Exemplar Essay 4

Discuss a drama which has a climax or a turning point.

"Othello" by William Shakespeare is a drama which focuses on the tragedy of Othello, a black General of the Venetian army who marries a white noblewoman. Yet, through the manipulations of his "ancient" (a trusted commander), Iago, Othello is consumed by the "green-eyed monster" of jealousy and kills his wife due to false accusations of adultery. Othello is the eponymous central character while the narrative pivots on the actions of the memorable Iago, a villain of the highest calibre. It is the death of Desdemona which represents the climax of this narrative, both in terms of action but also represents the success of Iago's scheming, the power of jealousy, but also marks the turning point into the downfall of Iago and his plans.

First, Shakespeare establishes this plotting arc and begins to set up the climax in Act 1 Scene 1 using imagery, "I follow him to serve my turn upon him". Iago, from the very opening, makes no secret to Roderigo (or the audience) of his intentions or his personality. He is very clear that he is a villain and wishes to do Othello harm ("serve my turn upon him"). The phrase "follow him" has connotations of back-stabbing while "serve" is ironic here because Iago appears to "serve" and be loyal, but "serve" in this context means to hurt. The word "upon" is also interesting

81

as it has connotations of falling and striking, like Iago is planning to hurt him with a weapon. This quotation clearly establishes the narrative arc of the play with "I follow him" showing Iago's duplicitous intentions and "to serve my turn upon him" indicating the eventually climax of Iago's revenge upon Othello. Notice that in Act 1 Iago's intentions are still vague. He is not specifically planning for the death of Desdemona but only for some non-specific "turn" or act of violence or betrayal. This clearly establishes the narrative arc that leads to the climax.

Within the same scene, Shakespeare uses imagery and repetition to create the characterisation of Iago which leads to the climax at the end, "I am not what I am". The repetition of the pronoun "I" shows Iago's selfish nature and that he only considers himself. The phrase "now what I am" establishes that Iago is duplicitous, a liar, and not what he seems. The irony in this sentence is that Iago is telling Roderigo the truth (that Iago is dangerous and not what he seems) but Roderigo still trusts him, not realising that Iago will also betray him - that Iago is also lying to him to get what he wants. Iago also ironically parodies God, whose names is 'I am who I am'. This makes Iago a Satan-like figure, an arch-villain and powerful manipulator. This sentence sems to establish that Iago's very nature (who he is as a person) is a large factor in what he is doing – that he is driven by his own evil to create the destruction to Othello. There are practical reasons Iago drives forward to the climax, but this line from Act 1 Scene 1 seems to imply a sense of inevitability to Desdemona's death as Iago has to follow his evil nature.

A main feature within the climax is Othello's anger and lack of self-control, which is established by Shakespeare in Act 2 Scene 3 using imagery, "if I once stir, or do but lift this arm, the best of you shall sink in my rebuke" Othello arrives and Iago helps him to break up the brawl between drunken Cassio and Roderigo – this makes Iago look calm and level-headed therefore building up Othello's trust in him for later. This is one of the first signs of Othello's lack of self-control around situations which is a character failing for later with Desdemona. The phrase "if I once stir" is a metaphor for him holding himself back. Othello means if that he starts to fight and hurt the men then he will do real violence ("sink in my rebuke"). Othello would probably be clenching his fist ("lift this arm") to emphasise the point. In fact, Othello uses nautical metaphors to describe the level of violence that he would inflict, comparing himself to a cannon that would "sink" a ship and "stir" has connotations of a storm or tempest that cannot be controlled once it is started. This emphasises Othello's role as a solider, but in a small manner plays into the racial stereotype of the anger, lack of self-control and violence of a black man. These are important features of Othello's character which Iago exploits to create the climax.

Shakespeare further moves Othello towards the final climax of the play using short sentences and suggestive statements, "Ha! I like not that." Iago and Othello in Act 3 Scene arrive on stage as Cassio is leaving after talking to Desdemona and Emilia. Iago has been waiting for this moment, a moment to suggest that there is something going on between Cassio and Desdemona. The exclamation of "Ha!" is ironic because Iago is using it catch Othello's attention and to suggest that he and Othello have 'caught' Cassio and Desdemona at something they shouldn't be. But it is also an expression of his own happiness that something that he has hoped for is coming so easily to him. The non-specific "that" is also interesting as Iago does not make it clear what he is talking about. He knows that Othello's jealousy will 'fill in the gaps' without needing to be specific. Iago is playing a careful and slow game, but one he is winning. He hammers home this suggestion in the next few lines by saying that Cassio "steals away so guilty-like". This is part of the slow build up to the climax and Othello's unravelling – one of the first steps in the slow suggestion of an affair that Iago builds up.

By the end of Act 3 Scene 3, Othello is using dark and destructive metaphors and imagery to describe his feelings towards Desdemona. The build up to the climax of her death has begun, "Even so my bloody thoughts, with violent pace, shall ne'er look back, ne'er ebb to humble love, till that a capable and wide revenge swallow them up". Iago has here mentioned that Cassio has Desdemona's handkerchief (which, of course, he does not) and this is the "ocular proof" that Othello demanded earlier. Notice Othello has yet to see this "proof" or ask for an explanation from Desdemona, but he is already discussing "bloody thoughts" (i.e. killing her). He has descended into his darkest thoughts quickly ("violent pace"). There is a sense in which Othello is acting before his love overwhelms him and he changes his mind, but it could also be part of the racist characterisation that the black man is so prone to violence and the lack of self-control we saw earlier. Othello's language has become dark and fierce ("bloody/violent") and also unstoppable ("pace/ne'er look back"). He balances "love" with "revenge", as if Desdemona has earned her death by making Othello love her and then betraying him. If Desdemona had committed adultery, then this was a crime that was punishable by law. But Othello doesn't not think along those lines - he wants "revenge" and not punishment. It is possible that Othello is reacting in this manner because he is a soldier and used to being "violent". He is also a very masculine character and being cuckolded (i.e. being cheated on and not knowing) was a huge embarrassment to a man's masculinity, something which a character like Othello could not bear. Desdemona also represented Othello's access to high Venetian society despite his race and so her betrayal with Cassio (which is of course false) represents his loss of place – especially as Desdemona would appear to be choosing a white man over him. Notice that this "revenge" that Othello is discussing is total and destructive, like a black hole ("swallow them up"). It is also interesting that Othello does not spare Cassio as the pronoun is plural: "them". Cassio will also be punished in this scenario. Othello wasn't just betrayed (he believes) by his wife, but also by a close friend and a subordinate in his own army. The climax is close at hand and there is a sense of Othello's character collapsing into his darkest thoughts as led by Iago.

By Act 4 Othello's anger has changed and grown, as reflected in Shakespeare's use of stage directions, "[Striking her] Devil!" This is Othello in Act 4, Scene 1. A letter arrives calling Othello home but promoting Cassio to the role of Governor of Cyprus. Desdemona says she is glad of his as she loves Cassio and Othello strikes her. The stage direction of "striking" is active,

84

violent and powerful and has connotations of the randomness and power of a lightning strike. It represents his resentment and power over her. It is also a word associated with animals (vipers and snakes) and weapons (swords) showing Othello's nature as a "beast" and soldier. The short sentence and exclamation of "devil" emphasise his belief that she is evil and beyond redemption. She is no longer even human anymore to him as her betrayal is so great. This is an easy verbal trick that Othello is using in order to dehumanise her in order to make killing her easier. The audience can see that Othello's rage has subsumed him and the climax (the death of Desdemona) is at hand.

The climax so long built up arrives in Act 5. Shakespeare emphasises the moment (and Desdemona's fear) through the use of exclamations, "Kill me to-morrow: let me live to-night!" Othello comes to Desdemona's chamber in Act 5 Scene 2 and makes it clear he will kill her for having an affair. Desdemona asks for Cassio to be brought in order to prove her innocence (notice that her word alone is not good enough) but Othello tells her that Cassio is dead. In Desdemona's fear she begs for her life – her desperation and fear of Othello can be seen in the exclamation mark. These represent the drama and violence of this moment of the play, just as he is about to strangle her. Notice that life and death are balanced in this sentence ("kill me ... let me live ...") just as Desdemona's life is balanced on the knife-edge of Othello's will. The climax of the play has arrived, and this is the point of choice for Othello – be a hero or a villain. Desdemona begs for even a little more time – a day, night, and even a half hour. She is hoping to put him off to earn more time for herself to prove her truth which is, in fact, exactly what she needed! In a few moments. the whole situation will unravel, and her honesty proved but Othello has acted too hastily, driven by jealousy: Othello kills Desdemona and the course of the play has been sealed as it almost inevitably seemed from the start.

The effects of the climax are emphasised by Shakespeare through metaphor and repetition in Othello's final lines, "I kiss'd thee ere I kill'd thee: no way but this; killing myself, to die upon a kiss." Othello stabs himself in Act 5 Scene 3 ("killing myself") and addresses his final lines to the corpse of Desdemona, which is still lying on the bed on the stage. The stage now has two dead bodies (Desdemona, Emilia) and three wounded (Cassio, Iago and Othello). The number of deaths and woundings are clear visual signals to the audience that the play is ending, and it is a tragedy. Othello, once again, speaks in doubles: "I kiss'd thee ere I kill'd thee". He means this literally, which is that he kissed Desdemona just before he strangled her. But, also, metaphorically, in that his love ("I kiss'd thee") was the cause of her death. If he had never met herm, and they had never fallen in love, then she would still be alive. His love was the cause of her death. Notice that he does show anger towards Iago, but these final lines do not seem to blame Iago – Othello is very much taking the blame upon himself. Would Othello still have killed Desdemona without Iago's "poison" and "pestilence"? It seems unlikely to the audience, but Othello here seems to imply that it was almost always destined to happen due to his love. There is also a sense of poetic justice for Othello in that his kiss brought her death and now he is dying and the last thing he will do is "die upon a kiss". The romantic and the tragic are here and now very much entangled. This has many striking similarities to *Romeo and Juliet*, which ends in a similar double-death of lovers. Shakespeare cleverly highlights this mixing of love and death for the audience through the use of alliteration and repetition: "kiss'd/kill'd/killing/kiss". This k-sound and use of consonance links the words within the audience's ear (they sound similar so they must be linked together) to further bring them together. Their similar sound linguistically links them through the use of sound techniques. The repetitive plosive k-sound (harsh, strong) also relates to the hash nature of both love and death. This is the final effect of the climax: to intermingle love and death.

In conclusion, "Othello" by William Shakespeare is a drama which creates and builds up to an effective and powerful climax: the death of Desdemona. The audience watches as Othello is manipulated and brought to a dark place by Iago, with Shakespeare showing us how easily our dark selves can be turned and how easily we can destroy what we love. The climax is a warning from Shakespeare – as is Othello's fate.

Exemplar Essay 5

Discuss a drama with an important theme (race/racism).

"Othello" by William Shakespeare is a drama which focuses on the tragedy of Othello, a black General of the Venetian army who marries a white noblewoman. Yet, through the manipulations of his "ancient" (a trusted commander), Iago, Othello is consumed by the "green-eyed monster" of jealousy and kills his wife due to false accusations of adultery. Othello is the eponymous central character, but this narrative also pivots and turns on the actions of the memorable Iago, a villain of the highest calibre who uses race against Othello as a weapon in his arsenal of manipulation. In fact, race and racism is an integral element and theme within this play, one which Shakespeare explores and exploits. Race is a central idea within the play – and a central driving force for the narrative itself, a function of the very play.

Shakespeare establishes race as an important theme within Act 1 Scene 1 through the use of racial stereotypes and insults, "the thicklips". Roderigo describes Othello here before the audience has met Othello and this, combined with mentions of "Moor" earlier in the scene, make it clear to the audience that Othello is non-white. This phrase shows Roderigo's disdain and racism for Othello, but remember Roderigo is also using racism in this context to describe a love rival. It is not purely racism that is motivating Roderigo. The use of the definite article "the" shows the audience that Roderigo only defines Othello by his blackness, that he others Othello and destroys his right to exist by reducing him to just the racial stereotype of "thicklips". Now Othello's actual race is hard to determine. The word "Moor" and even the word "black" do not have specific and fixed definitions for Shakespeare and his contemporary audience. Some uses of the word even just mean 'dark haired', swarthy or Mediterranean in origin. It is a general term which shifts, especially in the absence of much ethnic diversity. Yet the use of this term "thicklips" has specific racial stereotypes of Sub-Saharan African descent. It is hard to establish Shakespeare's particular views from those of the characters. Does the use of the racial slur in his play make Shakespeare racist? Well, it is Roderigo who uses it, a character the audience is not supposed to like, and this dislike is being emphasised by his racism. Shakespeare seems to indicate that racism is a negative quality to be avoided. Shakespeare is also using common terminology of his period, words and phrases that would not be out of place. Can we assign a modern value judgement to something written such a long time ago in a very different context? These are questions still struggle with to this day.

Shakespeare further emphasises the racism of Venetian society and Iago's use of race as a weapon in Act 1 Scene 1 through the use of a metaphor, "an old black ram is tupping your white ewe". Iago and Roderigo go to Brabantio's window – Desdemona's father – and call up to him. They intend on telling Brabantio about Othello and Desdemona's marriage to cause mischief and begin by calling out "thieves" to rouse him, implying that he has been robbed (meaning Desdemona is property stolen). Iago uses a negative sexual image. In this case Othello is the "black ram", Desdemona is the "white ewe", and "tupping" is sexual intercourse or rape. This entire image is laced with racism – and deliberately so as Iago wishes to anger Brabantio. Notice that "tupping" is Iago reducing Othello and Desdemona's love to a sexual and animalistic component. The inter-racial relationship between the two characters is turned into something bestial, inhumane, and to be found disgusting.

This is further highlighted by the equating of Othello with a "ram", an animal. Othello is being denied his humanity. The "ram" is also associated with the devil and evil, with a "black ram" being one of the ways that the Devil could appear on Earth in Shakespeare's audience's mind. Othello is being associated with evil and the Devil, as he is later by Brabantio who accuses him of witchcraft. The "ram" is also associated with sexual appetites and being out of control (also a stereotype of black men) and so the racism is further layered. Iago emphasises this situation by bringing to the fore Desdemona's whiteness – "white ewe". Iago wishes to build the image and contrast of "black" and "white" to anger Brabantio. Where "black ram" dehumanises Othello, "white" has associations of purity and innocence. The "white ewe" was also a costly creature so showing importance and worth, hence why it is important to be protected. The word "black" has the opposite connotations to a Shakespearean audience and so Iago is implying that Othello's evil is inherent to his very skin-colour and race, a very racist idea. Ultimately, Desdemona is also reduced to property and an animal in this sentence. Although she is an 'important' animal to Brabantio, she and Othello still occupy a lower status in the power hierarchy of the play (although she is above Othello). It is very clear here that racism is a feature of Venetian society and the inter-racial marriage of Othello and Desdemona, although not illegal, horrifies the rich Brabantio: Iago plays on the racism within society in order to work his manipulations and evil. Yet it is hard to know if Iago himself is actually racist in the sense of disliking Othello for his racial background, or if Iago is using systemic racism to punish Othello. Ultimately the language Iago uses and outcome he achieves are the same regardless of intention and beliefs: Iago destroys the life of a black man using his blackness against him. Whether or not he actual holds racist views, Iago acts like a racist and, as with Roderigo, Iago is presented as a villain associated with witchcraft, the Devil and evil so his use of racism and racist language is definitely presented as wrong-doing. Form this the audience can infer that Shakespeare's message in the play is supposed to be overtly anti-racist and overtly tolerant of the inter-racial marriage.

Yet, Shakespeare does rely on racial stereotypes that make the play problematic to a modern audience, "Even so my bloody thoughts, with violent pace, shall ne'er look back, ne'er ebb to humble love, till that a capable and wide revenge swallow them up". In Act 3 Scene 3 Iago mentions that Cassio has Desdemona's handkerchief (which, of course, he does not) and this is apparently the "ocular proof" that Othello demanded. Notice Othello has yet to see this "proof" or ask for an explanation from Desdemona, but he is already discussing "bloody thoughts" (i.e. killing her). He has descended into his darkest thoughts quickly ("violent pace"). His language has become dark and fierce ("bloody/violent") and also unstoppable ("pace/ne'er look back"). There is a sense in which Othello is acting before his love overwhelms him and he changes his mind, but it is also part of a racist characterisation that a black man is prone to violence and lacks control. Shakespeare is using this stereotype of black violence as a reason that Othello is willing to kill Desdemona – Shakespeare both criticises this idea (by having Iago use it) but he also uses it to further his plot and narrative along. Yet it is possible that Othello is reacting in this manner because he is a soldier and used to being "violent". He is also a very masculine character and being cuckolded (i.e. being cheated on and not knowing) was a huge embarrassment to a man's masculinity, something which a character like Othello could not bear. Desdemona also represented Othello's access to high Venetian society and so her betrayal with Cassio (which is of course false) represents his loss of reputation – especially as Desdemona would appear to be choosing a white man over him. Ultimately, the answer to Othello's violence is a combination of the above. This is what makes Shakespeare such a complex writer and Othello such a complex character: the variety of motivations that push forward Othello and make the unimaginable (killing his beloved Desdemona) a realistic option by the end of the play. We are then left with the strange dichotomy: is Othello a complex black character with multiple motivations or is he just another example in literature of the 'angry, violent black man'? Is Shakespeare reflecting a racist society or is his writing racist?

In Act 4 Shakespeare presents us with a possible answer to this issue with Othello's use of a metaphor, "A horned man's a monster and a beast". Here Othello describes himself as a "horned man", a reference to the Jacobean idea of a cuckold. This is a man whose wife is openly cheating on him and he is deceived by her. This is metaphorically represented as a man with stag antlers, which is humiliating to the man, both personally and socially. In this case, Othello takes his perceived state of being a cuckold and transfers it into being a "beast" and a "monster", a devil with horns. Othello is taking something passive (a cuckold) and creating a violent active state (a demon) – specifically a state of being with violent power, a power reminiscent of his earlier status and masculine power as a solider. Othello would rather be a murdering "beast" than mocked cuckold. Othello seems to be degrading himself (implying that Desdemona has transformed him into a "beast") and it is possible that Othello is trying to dehumanise himself to justify the anger and violence he is about to commit, separate himself from his humanity to protect himself. Ultimately, Othello seems to be creating a narrative to himself about who he is – he is internalising the racist idea of a black man being a "beast" that was held in Venetian society. This is a rather complex idea: Othello is acting like the racist stereotype that he is expected to be. The society that he is living in has rejected his attempt to integrate and be seen as equal (marrying Desdemona) and, so, Othello attempts to be become what achieved success for him before (the violent soldier) and the thing that society expects of him ("beast"). Shakespeare is therefore not revealing himself to be racist in his creation of Othello but is, in fact, showing the corrupting force of racism within a society: we create the "monster" and "beast" that we fear when we reject the humanity of others.

Ultimately, this "beast" is all that Venetian society will see, which is exemplified by Shakespeare in Act 5 Scene 2 through the use of metaphors, "the more angel she, and you the blacker devil!" After Othello admits to killing Desdemona, Emilia curses him. She calls him a "devil", implying that he is evil and full of sin. There is a sense in which he damned by his very existence and nothing he can say will save him now. She also raises his race ("blacker"). She uses it as if it is evidence of his evil and notice that it is a comparative adjective ("blacker") used, implying that Othello is the worst of humanity and darker than Satan himself. His evil is absolute. This "blacker" also highlights the difference between Othello and Desdemona by calling her an "angel", which has associations of purity and whiteness. Remember Desdemona is also surrounded by her wedding sheets (that would be white) and these may also look like angel's wings, highlighting the spiritual and physical differences between Othello and Desdemona. There is a total reduction in this moment of the complexity of Othello and his motivations (the racism, the ostracization from society, the foreground of violence in his life) as Emilia reduces the situation to a basic narrative of good versus evil which Venetian society will understand. Notice also that Emilia, only a few lines previous, was in favour of Desdemona and Othello's love in the broadest sense. She switches to this racist and reduced view of Othello very quickly, implying the underlying racist ideology she held about Othello but was unwilling to show until this moment. There is a sense in which Shakespeare is showing a world in which the racist ideology of 'blackness is evil' is a hidden element but is quick to emerge when allowed, an idea which is perhaps still reflected in the modern world.

Interestingly it is this idea of narrative and storytelling which Othello comes back to just before he kills himself in Act 5 Scene 2, "when you shall these unlucky deeds relate, speak of me as I am; nothing extenuate, nor set down aught in malice". During his final confession, Othello speaks of himself in a vaguely past tense manner ("these unlucky deeds relate"), a verbal cue that he plans to kill himself. Yet he asks for fair judgement ("speak of me as I am"): he does not wish actions to be downplayed ("nothing extenuate") nor does he wish to be a devil ("nor set down aught in malice"). It is the story/narrative (and, therefore, his reputation and how he is remembered) which Othello is concerned about. There is sense of trying to control history post his death, as well as bring nuance and subtlety to what Othello knows will be a basic understanding of events. Othello fears Emilia (and others like her) and how they will interpret his actions. He wishes for his complexity and humanity (both good and bad) to be remembered. Othello fears the reduction of his acts to 'black men are violent and so Othello killed his wife' (which, in fact, reinforces racism) and, instead, wishes the full story to be told in which he is a human being. He does not excuse his acts but does not want them reduced purely to his race. He also takes responsibility for his actions, not attempting to shift blame to Iago (where much of it rightly lies) which ennobles him in those final moments of his life.

In conclusion, "Othello" by William Shakespeare is a drama which presents an important and powerful theme – that of race and racism. "Othello" has always been a problematic text for this particular theme, not least because the play has a long history of Othello being played by white men in blackface. A play is more than just a piece of writing and, so, if we are considering racism within a play we must look not just at the playwright and characters but also direction, actors and stage craft. A modern audience cannot escape the inherent racism in a blackface presentation of Othello. So, what is Shakespeare's message tucked within this play? Does he present a fundamentally racist story and view of the world? From far away, it may seem so – a violent black man kills his wife in an incredibly racist society. This seems to reinforce stereotypes and abuse those stereotypes, presenting little hope. Yet, we must acknowledge Shakespeare's genius and defer to his words, as spoken by Othello: "speak of me as I am; nothing extenuate, nor set down aught in malice". Surely the complexity, grace and nobility of Othello must also count for something, some sort of balance to the darkness.

Printed in Great Britain
by Amazon